ETERNAL SECURITY

GERALD MCDANIEL

WESTBOW°
PRESS
A DIVISION OF THOMAS NELSON
& ZONDERVAN

Scripture taken from the King James Version of the Bible.

WestBow Press books may be ordered through
booksellers or by contacting:

WestBow Press
A Division of Thomas Nelson & Zondervan
1663 Liberty Drive
Bloomington, IN 47403
www.westbowpress.com
1 (866) 928-1240

ISBN: 978-1-4908-3116-9 (sc)

Library of Congress Control Number: 2014905483

Printed in the United States of America.

WestBow Press rev. date: 03/19/2014

Contents

Chapter 1

<u>The Plan of Salvation</u>

Let's go through **4 H's. Honesty, Humility, Helpless and Hope**

H   #1) *You must be **HONEST** enough to admit you have sinned and broken God's commands. Understand in doing so, this puts you in very great danger!*

Romans 3:10 "there is none righteous, no not one"

Romans 3:23 "...all have sinned..."

I John 1:8 "if we say that we have no sin, we deceive ourselves, and the truth is not in us"

H   #2) *You must be **HUMBLE** enough to admit you deserve Hell when you die.*
One sin disqualifies us from Heaven and we have all sinned more than once.

Romans 6:23 "For the wages of sin [is] death"

Revelation 21:8 "But the fearful, and unbelieving, and the abominable, and murderers, and whoremongers, and sorcerers, and idolaters, and all liars, shall have their part in the lake which burneth with fire and brimstone: which is the second death"

H   #3) *You must understand you are **HELPLESS** when it comes to you saving yourself from going to Hell*

Gerald McDaniel

when you die. There is nothing you can do to pay for your own sin.

Ephesians 2:8-9 For by grace are ye saved through faith; and that not of yourselves: it is the gift of God: not of works, lest any man should boast.

Titus 3:5 Not by works of righteousness which we have done, but according to his mercy he saved us, by the washing of regeneration, and renewing of the Holy Ghost;

Galatians 2:16 Knowing that a man is not justified by the works of the law, but by the faith of Jesus Christ, even we have believed in Jesus Christ, that we might be justified by the faith of Christ, and not by the works of the law: for by the works of the law shall no flesh be justified.

Understand when I say HELPLESS it means you cannot surrender your life to Christ for salvation. You have no life to surrender. You are dead in trespasses and sins. You cannot yet make Jesus the Lord of your life because you have no life. Jesus will not be Lord of your life until He is Savior of your soul. You cannot turn from your sins because you are dead in your sins. You must see yourself HELPLESS at the Mercy of God. Now you are ready for H # 4.

H #4) *You are helpless but not hopeless. Your **HOPE** must be in Jesus, God's Son and what he has done for you on the cross when He died there. Jesus is the only one that paid for your sins when he died on the cross.*

He was buried and arose again. You must ask Jesus to be your personal Savior and ask Jesus to save you from Hell. If you are depending on church membership to save you that means you are not depending on Jesus to save you. If you are depending on the good deeds you do to save you, that means you are not depending on Jesus to save you. If you are depending on baptism to save you that means you are not depending on Jesus to save you. It must be Jesus and what Jesus did for you on the cross that you are depending on to save you. Nothing else can go with this. Jesus is the only one that paid for your sins on the cross so Jesus is the only one that can save you.

Romans 5:8 But God commendeth his love toward us, in that, while we were yet sinners, Christ died for us.

I Peter 3:18 For Christ also hath once suffered for sins, the just for the unjust, that he might bring us to God, being put to death in the flesh but quickened by the Spirit.

Hebrews 10:12 But this man (JESUS) after he hath offered one sacrifice for sins for ever, sat down on the right hand of God.

John 14:6 Jesus saith unto him, I am the way, the truth, and the life: no man cometh unto the Father, but by me.

Acts 4:12 Neither is there salvation in any other: for there is none other name under heaven given among men, whereby we must be saved.

John 3:16 For God so loved the world, that he gave his only begotten Son, that whosoever believeth in him should not perish, but have everlasting life.

Ask Jesus to save you before it is too late:

Romans 10:13 For whosoever shall call upon the name of the Lord shall be saved.

Chapter 2

Some General Verses on Eternal Security
(It is impossible to lose your salvation.)

Note: The one false teaching that Satan has used to attempt to bridge the gap between the false religions and the true religion is the false doctrine of "losing your salvation". Most people that teach you can lose your salvation teach you have to work to keep your salvation or work to get your salvation. So they are relying on their works to get them to heaven instead of Jesus and what Jesus did for them on the cross of Calvary. This means they are still lost. They take passages out of context, trying to make them say you have to work your way into heaven and that you can lose your salvation.

1) **We receive eternal life immediately upon trusting in Jesus Christ as Savior and not after you die as some would have you to believe.**

John 3:15 That whosoever believeth in him should not perish, but <u>have eternal life.</u>

John 3:16 For God so loved the world, that he gave his only begotten Son, that whosoever believeth in him should not perish, but <u>have everlasting life.</u>

John 3:36 He that believeth on the Son <u>hath everlasting life</u>: and he that believeth not the Son shall not see life; but the wrath of God abideth on him.

John 5:24 Verily, verily, I say unto you, He that heareth my word, and believeth on him that sent me, <u>hath everlasting life</u>, and shall not come into condemnation; but is passed from death unto life.

John 6:40 And this is the will of him that sent me, that every one which seeth the Son, and believeth on him, may <u>have everlasting life</u>: and I will raise him up at the last day.

John 6:47 Verily, verily, I say unto you, He that believeth on me <u>hath everlasting life</u>.

John 10:28 And <u>I give unto them eternal life</u>; and they shall never perish, neither shall any [man] pluck them out of my hand.

1 John 5:13 These things have I written unto you that believe on the name of the Son of God; <u>that ye may know that ye have eternal life</u>, and that ye may believe on the name of the Son of God.

2) Eternal life is given to us as a promise from God.

1 John 2:25 And this is the promise that he hath promised us, [even] eternal life.

Titus 1:2 In hope of eternal life, which God, that cannot lie, promised before the world began;

3) Eternal life is given to us as a present from God.

Romans 6:23 For the wages of sin [is] death; but the gift of God [is] eternal life through Jesus Christ our Lord.

4) When we trust Christ as our personal Savior we are sealed unto the day of redemption.

Eph. 1:13 In whom ye also [trusted], after that ye heard the word of truth, the gospel of your salvation: in whom also after that ye believed, ye were sealed with that holy Spirit of promise,

Eph. 1:14 Which is the earnest of our inheritance until the redemption of the purchased possession, unto the praise of his glory.

Eph. 4:30 And grieve not the holy Spirit of God, whereby ye are sealed unto the day of redemption.

5) When we trust Christ as our personal Savior we are preserved forever.

Psalm 37:28 For the LORD loveth judgment, and forsaketh not his saints; they are preserved for ever: but the seed of the wicked shall be cut off.

6) Nothing can separate us from the love of God.

Rom. 8:38 For I am persuaded, that neither death, nor life, nor angels, nor principalities, nor powers, nor things present, nor things to come,

Rom. 8:39 Nor height, nor depth, nor any other creature, shall be able to separate us from the love of God, which is in Christ Jesus our Lord.

7) There is no condemnation to those who have trusted in Christ as Savior.

Rom. 8:1 [There is] therefore now no condemnation to them which are in Christ Jesus, who walk not after the flesh, but after the Spirit.

John 3:18 He that believeth on him is not condemned: but he that believeth not is condemned already, because he hath not believed in the name of the only begotten Son of God.

8) When we trust Christ as our personal Savior we will never be cast out.

John 6:37 All that the Father giveth me shall come to me; and him that cometh to me I will in no wise cast out.

Psalm 37:23 The steps of a [good] man are ordered by the LORD: and he delighteth in his way.

Psalm 37:24 Though he fall, he shall not be utterly cast down: for the LORD upholdeth [him with] his hand.

9) God is able to keep us from falling.

Jude 24 Now unto him that is able to keep you from falling, and to present [you] faultless before the presence of his glory with exceeding joy,

10) God promised to conform us into the image of Christ.

Romans 8:29 For whom he did foreknow, he also did predestinate [to be] conformed to the image of his Son, that he might be the firstborn among many brethren.

11) God will never forsake those who have trusted Jesus Christ as Savior.

Hebrews 13:5 [Let your] conversation [be] without covetousness; [and be] content with such things as ye have: for he hath said, I will never leave thee, nor forsake thee.

Psalm 37:28 For the LORD loveth judgment, and forsaketh not his saints; They are preserved for ever: but the seed of the wicked shall be cut off.

12) Our punishment for sin changed from Hell to chastisement after we trusted Christ as our personal Savior. This

rules out the notion that because we are eternally secure that we have a ticket or a freedom to sin.

1 Cor. 11:32 But when we are judged, we are chastened of the Lord, that we should not be condemned with the world.

Psalm 89:31 If they break my statutes, and keep not my commandments;

Psalm 89:32 Then will I visit their transgression with the rod, and their iniquity with stripes.

Psalm 89:33 Nevertheless my lovingkindness will I not utterly take from him, nor suffer my faithfulness to fail.

Psalm 89:34 My covenant will I not break, nor alter the thing that is gone out of my lips.

13) No one is able to take us out of God's hand.

John 10:28 And I give unto them eternal life; and they shall never perish, neither shall any [man] pluck them out of my hand.

John 10:29 My Father, which gave [them] me, is greater than all; and no [man] is able to pluck [them] out of my Father's hand.

14) No one is able to add to or take away from what God has done for those who have trusted Christ as Savior.

Eccl. 3:14 I know that, whatsoever God doeth, it shall be for ever: nothing can be put to it, nor any thing taken from it: and God doeth [it], that [men] should fear before him.

15) Those who have trusted Christ as Savior may not have any good works to show at the Judgment Seat but they are still saved. (You may lose your rewards but you cannot lose your salvation.)

1 Cor. 3:15 If any man's work shall be burned, he shall suffer loss: but he himself shall be saved; yet so as by fire.

2 John 8 Look to yourselves, that we lose not those things which we have wrought, but that we receive a full reward.

16) The work that God started in us when we trusted Christ as Savior will be performed until the day of Christ. This tells us that God will never give up on us.

Phil. 1:6 Being confident of this very thing, that he which hath begun a good work in you will perform [it] until the day of Jesus Christ:

17) Our citizenship is put in heaven when we trust Christ as our personal Savior.

Phil. 3:20 For our conversation is in heaven; from whence also we look for the Saviour, the Lord Jesus Christ:

Eph. 2:19 Now therefore ye are no more strangers and foreigners, but fellowcitizens with the saints, and of the household of God;

18) God saves us to the uttermost.

Heb. 7:25 Wherefore he is able also to save them to the uttermost that come unto God by him, seeing he ever liveth to make intercession for them.

19) Trusting Christ as our personal Savior is how we overcome the world.

1 John 5:4 For whatsoever is born of God overcometh the world: and this is the victory that overcometh the world, [even] our faith.

1 John 5:5 Who is he that overcometh the world, but he that believeth that Jesus is the Son of God?

20) Because we have overcome by faith we will not be hurt of the second death. The

second death is spending eternity in the lake of fire.

Rev. 2:11 He that hath an ear, let him hear what the Spirit saith unto the churches; He that overcometh shall not be hurt of the second death.

21) Because we have overcome by faith our name will not be blotted out of the book of life.

Rev. 3:5 He that overcometh, the same shall be clothed in white raiment; and I will not blot out his name out of the book of life, but I will confess his name before my Father, and before his angels.

22) Those who have trusted Christ as Savior are kept by the power of God.

1 Peter 1:3 Blessed [be] the God and Father of our Lord Jesus Christ, which according to his abundant mercy hath begotten us again unto a lively hope by the resurrection of Jesus Christ from the dead,

1 Peter 1:4 To an inheritance incorruptible, and undefiled, and that fadeth not away, reserved in heaven for you,

1 Peter 1:5 Who are kept by the power of God through faith unto salvation ready to be revealed in the last time.

23) God is faithful and He has promised us, so there is no need of doubting our salvation.

Hebrews 10:23 Let us hold fast the profession of [our] faith without wavering; (for he [is] faithful that promised;)

24) God is able to keep that which we have committed unto Him against that day.

2 Tim. 1:12 For the which cause I also suffer these things: nevertheless I am not ashamed: for I know whom I have believed, and am persuaded that he is able to keep that which I have committed unto him against that day.

Chapter 3

<u>Thou Hast the Words of Eternal Life</u>

John 6:67-69 Then said Jesus unto the twelve, Will ye also go away? **68** Then Simon Peter answered him, Lord, to whom shall we go? <u>thou hast the words of eternal life.</u> **69** And we believe and are sure that thou art that Christ, the Son of the living God.

I. Eternal life is given to us by God immediately when we trust Christ as our personal Savior.

John 3:15 That whosoever believeth in him should not perish, <u>but have eternal life</u>.

John 3:16 For God so loved the world, that he gave his only begotten Son, that whosoever believeth in him should not perish, <u>but have everlasting life</u>.

John 3:36 He that believeth on the Son <u>hath everlasting life</u>: and he that believeth not the Son shall not see life; but the wrath of God abideth on him.

John 5:24 Verily, verily, I say unto you, He that heareth my word, and believeth on him that sent me, <u>hath everlasting life</u>, and shall not come into condemnation; but is passed from death unto life.

John 6:40 And this is the will of him that sent me, that everyone which seeth the Son, and believeth on him, <u>may have everlasting life</u>: and I will raise him up at the last day.

John 6:47 Verily, verily, I say unto you, He that believeth on me <u>hath everlasting life</u>.

John 10:28 And <u>I give unto them eternal life</u>; and they shall never perish, neither shall any *man* pluck them out of my hand.

Act 13:48 And when the Gentiles heard this, they were glad, and glorified the word of the Lord: and as many as were ordained to eternal life believed.

Rom 6:23 For the wages of sin *is* death; but <u>the gift of God *is* eternal life</u> through Jesus Christ our Lord.

1Ti 1:16 Howbeit for this cause I obtained mercy, that in me first Jesus Christ might shew forth all longsuffering, for a pattern to them which should hereafter believe on him to life everlasting.

1Jo 2:25 And this is the promise that he hath promised us, *even* eternal life.

1Jo 5:13 These things have I written unto you that believe on the name of the Son of God<u>; that ye may know that ye have eternal life</u>, and that ye may believe on the name of the Son of God.

Sometimes the phrase "eternal life" or "everlasting life" is used in the Bible for something besides eternal salvation. Note the following:

1) Jesus is called eternal life. (I John 1:2)

(For the life was manifested, and we have seen it, and bear witness, and shew unto you that eternal life, which was with the Father, and was manifested unto us;)

(1 John 5:20) (And we know that the Son of God is come, and hath given us an understanding, that we may know him that is true, and we are in him that is true, [even] in his Son Jesus Christ. This is the true God, and eternal life.)

2) The Bible is called eternal life.

(John 12:50)(And I know that his commandment is life everlasting: whatsoever I speak therefore, even as the Father said unto me, so I speak.)

(1 John 5:11)(And this is the record, that God hath given to us eternal life, and this life is in his Son.)

3) Our rewards in heaven are called eternal life.

(John 4:36)(And he that reapeth receiveth wages, and gathereth fruit unto life eternal: that both he that soweth and he that reapeth may rejoice together.)

(John 6:27)(Labour not for the meat which perisheth, but for that meat which endureth unto everlasting life, which the Son of man shall give unto you: for him hath God the Father sealed.)

Notice the following verses on an example of eternal rewards.

Romans 2:7-10
Eternal Rewards for the Saved

7 To them who by patient continuance in well doing seek for glory and honour and immortality, eternal life:

Note: Here eternal life is not referring to salvation, in many other places it does. [Example] John 3:15-16, 36; 5:24; 6:40, 47; 10:28; Rom. 6:23; I Tim. 1:16; I John 2:25; 5:13 all refer to salvation.

1) *Jesus is called eternal life. (I John 1:2) (For the life was manifested, and we have seen it, and bear witness, and shew unto you that eternal life, which was with the Father, and was manifested unto us;)*

(1 John 5:20) (And we know that the Son of God is come, and hath given us an understanding, that we may know him that is true, and we are in him that is true, [even] in his Son Jesus Christ. This is the true God, and eternal life.)

2) *The bible is called eternal life.*

(John 12:50)(And I know that his commandment is life everlasting: whatsoever I speak therefore, even as the Father said unto me, so I speak.)
(1 John 5:11)(And this is the record, that God hath given to us eternal life, and this life is in his Son.)

3) *Our rewards in heaven are called eternal life.*

(John 4:36)(And he that reapeth receiveth wages, and gathereth fruit unto life eternal: that both he that soweth and he that reapeth may rejoice together.)

(John 6:27)(Labour not for the meat which perisheth, but for that meat which endureth unto everlasting life, which the Son of man shall give unto you: for him hath God the Father sealed.)

Note: Eternal life in 'Rom. 2:7' is referring to eternal rewards for the true believer who "by patient continuance in well doing seek for glory and honour and immortality"

Eternal Damnation for the Lost

8 But unto them that are contentious, and do not obey the truth, but obey unrighteousness, indignation and wrath,

9 Tribulation and anguish, upon every soul of man that doeth evil, of the Jew first, and also of the Gentile;

Note: v. 8-9 is referring to eternal degrees of punishment to the unbeliever who "are contentious, and do not obey the truth, but obey unrighteousness" they are promised "indignation and wrath, tribulation and anguish, upon every soul of man that doeth evil."

Eternal Rewards to the Saved

10 But glory, honour, and peace, to every man that worketh good, to the Jew first, and also to the Gentile:

Note: This verse is talking to saved people. We cannot expect lost people to work good.

Some people think that there are certain things you can do to try to earn eternal life. Notice the question asked in the following verses.

Mat 19:16 And, behold, one came and said unto him, <u>Good Master, what good thing shall I do, that I may have eternal life?</u>

Mat 19:17 And he said unto him, Why callest thou me good? *there is* none good but one, *that is*, God: but if thou wilt enter into life, keep the commandments.

Note: Jesus is not saying here that Jesus Himself is bad. He is talking to an individual that believes that all Jesus is, is a good master. The man did not realize that he was talking to God. So Jesus asked him why call him just a good master. In the human race all have sinned and if the man thinks that Jesus is just a good master, this means the man must think that Jesus is a sinner, no matter how good.

Note: Jesus said if he will enter into life to keep the commandments. If you can keep the commandments you can have eternal life. The point is Jesus just told him that there is none good but one, that is, God and now the man is trying to claim he has kept God's commands.

Mat 19:18 He saith unto him, Which? Jesus said, Thou shalt do no murder, Thou shalt not commit adultery, Thou shalt not steal, Thou shalt not bear false witness,

Note: It would take a lot of arrogance to ask Jesus which commands should I keep and evidently break the others. When Jesus says "thou shalt not bear false witness" notice the statement in **Romans 3:4** *God forbid: yea, let God be true, but **every man a liar**; as it is written, That thou mightest be justified in thy sayings, and mightest overcome when thou art judged. According to this everyone has lied.*

James 2:10 *For whosoever shall keep the whole law, and yet offend in one point, he is guilty of all.*

Mat 19:19 Honour thy father and *thy* mother: and, Thou shalt love thy neighbour as hyself.

Mat 19:20 The young man saith unto him, All these things have I kept from my youth up: what lack I yet?

Note: The young man claims the impossible. He says he has kept all these commands from his youth.

Mat 19:21 Jesus said unto him, **If** thou wilt be perfect, go *and* sell that thou hast, and give to the poor, and thou shalt have treasure in heaven: and come *and* follow me.

*Note: Jesus says **"IF THOU WILT BE PERFECT"**. If the young man was perfect he would have no problem with selling all he had and giving to the poor and following Jesus. If the man were perfect he would have no sins that must be paid for. **He refused to see himself a hell deserving lost sinner so he also saw no need for a Savior.***

Mat 19:22 But when the young man heard that saying, he went away sorrowful: for he had great possessions.

Mat 19:23 Then said Jesus unto his disciples, Verily I say unto you, <u>That a rich man shall hardly enter into the kingdom of heaven.</u>

Note: Jesus is not saying it is a sin to be rich. Many of God's people in the Old Testament times were rich. Example: Abraham; Isaac; Jacob; Lot; David; Solomon; Josiah; Hezekiah; and many others. However a lot of rich people are depending on and trusting in their riches for salvation instead of Jesus.

Mat 19:24 And again I say unto you, It is easier for a camel to go through the eye of a needle, than for a rich man to enter into the kingdom of God.

Mat 19:25 When his disciples heard *it*, they were exceedingly amazed, saying, **<u>Who then can be saved?</u>**

Mat 19:26 But Jesus beheld *them*, and said unto them, **<u>With men this is impossible</u>**; but with God all things are possible.

*Note: It is impossible for men to save themselves. This is why we must trust Jesus Christ for our salvation. V.26 **Jesus said with men this is impossible**.*

What about the verses that speaks of laying hold on eternal life?

1 Timothy 6:12 Fight the good fight of faith, <u>lay hold on eternal life</u>, whereunto thou art also called, and hast professed a good profession before many witnesses.

1 Timothy 6:19 Laying up in store for themselves a good foundation against the time to come, that they may <u>lay hold on eternal life</u>.

These verses are referring to claiming the promise of eternal life and not doubting your salvation. We must recognize that eternal life is ours as a <u>gift from God</u> when we trust Christ as our personal Savior.

Romans 6:23 For the wages of sin *is* death; but the gift of God *is* eternal life through Jesus Christ our Lord.

We must recognize that eternal life is a <u>promise from God</u> to all that trust Jesus Christ as their personal Savior.

1 John 2:25 And this is the promise that he hath promised us, *even* eternal life.

<u>God wants us to know</u> that we are given eternal life immediately upon trusting Christ as our personal Savior.

1 John 5:13 These things have I written unto you that believe on the name of the Son of God; **<u>that ye may know that ye have eternal life</u>**, and that ye may believe on the name of the Son of God.

Chapter 4

Some Verses in the Bible if taken out of Context, Seem to Suggest that you can Lose your Salvation

I.   Heb. 5:14-6:10

The Matured in Christ

Heb. 5:14 But strong meat belongeth to them that are of <u>full age</u>, [even] those who by reason of use have their <u>senses</u> exercised to discern both good and evil.

Note: "full age" #5046 (19x)(perfect-17; men; of full age)]
Note: "senses" [145][1 time][def. judgment]
Note: The more we learn the more we can understand to learn even more and teach and be better at discerning between good and evil.

Heb. Chapter 6
Building on the Foundation

1 Therefore leaving the <u>principles</u> of the doctrine of Christ, let us go on unto perfection; not laying again the foundation of repentance from dead works, and of faith toward God,

Note: "principles" #746 (58x)(beginnings-40; principality-8; corner-2; first-2; misc-6)

Note: "leaving the principles of the doctrine of Christ" does not mean to abandon them, it means to build on top of or above these principles just like framing a building on a foundation.

2 Of the doctrine of baptisms, and of laying on of hands, and of resurrection of the dead, and of eternal judgment.

3 And this will we do, if God permit.

To Whom Much is Given, Much is Required

4 For [it is] impossible for those who were once enlightened, and have tasted of the heavenly gift, and <u>were made partakers of the Holy Ghost,</u>

Note: "enlightened" (#5461)()11x)(give light 2; bring to light 2; lighten 2; enlighten 2; light; illuminate; make to see)

Note: "have tasted" (#1089)(15 x)(taste-12; have eaten-3) (<u>Heb. 2:9</u>-Jesus tasted

death for every man)

Note: "were made partakers of the Holy Ghost" means there was a genuine conversion.

Note: "partakers" #3353 (6x)(partaker-4; partner <u>Luke 5:7</u>; fellow)

5 And have tasted the good word of God, and the powers of the world to come,

Note: These are not only believers but also believers with maturity and have been given leadership positions and responsibilities.

6 If they shall **fall away**, to **renew** them again unto repentance; seeing they crucify to themselves the Son of God afresh, and put [him] to an open shame.

Note: "fall away" [#3895 -1 time- def. deviate from right path][not the same as in II Thess. 2:3 (646-"apostasia")(fall away; forsake-Acts 21:21)]
Note: "renew" [340 -1 time- def. renovate] [this does not mean forgive]
Note: "open shame"[#3856 -2 times- 1 time Mat. 1:19 "make a public example"]
Note: The falling away here is not apostasy. It is a matured responsible believer who is getting off on the wrong path and in to open sin and losing his position of service. It is impossible to get that position of service back.

7 For the earth which drinketh in the rain that cometh oft upon it, and bringeth forth herbs meet for them by whom it is dressed, receiveth blessing from God:

Note: This is not two different kinds of ground, it is two different kinds of plants coming from the one ground. (good and bad)(herbs and thorns & briers)

8 But that which beareth thorns and briers [is] rejected, and [is] nigh unto cursing; whose end [is] to be burned.

Note: v. 8 "burned" is referring to the fire at the Judgment Seat of Christ.

1 Corinthians 3:12-15
12 Now if any man build upon this foundation gold, silver, precious stones, wood, hay, stubble;

13 Every man's work shall be made manifest: for the day shall declare it, because it shall be <u>revealed by fire</u>; and <u>the fire</u> shall try every man's work of what sort it is.

14 If any man's work abide which he hath built thereupon, he shall receive a reward.

15 If any man's <u>work shall be burned</u>, he shall suffer loss: but he himself shall be saved; yet so as <u>by fire</u>.

Note: At the Judgment Seat Of Christ [herbs as 'gold, silver, or precious stone' and thorns & briers as 'wood, hay, and stubble] **<u>When you burn a field off, you are not doing it to destroy the ground but to purge the ground</u>** *from briers etc.*
Note: This passage not only refers to saved people: v. 4 "were made partakers of the Holy Ghost" but also matured Christians. 6:1 "let us go on to perfection" & Heb.5:14 "But strong meat belongeth to them that are of full age"
Note: Bible examples:

1) Saul:
   a. Partaker of the Holy Spirit with great responsibilities.(I Sam. 10:6,9-10; 11:6)
   b. His falling away (I Sam. 13:9, 12-13; 15:9, 11)
   c. Impossible to restore him to being King again (I Sam. 15:11; 16:1; 28:19-20)

2) *Moses*
   a. *Partaker of the Holy Spirit with great responsibilities.*
   b. *His falling away (Num. 20:8, 10-12)*
   c. *His impossibility to lead children of Israel into Promised Land (Num. 20:12; Deut. 34:4)*

3) *Man of God in I Kings 13*
   a. *Partaker of the Holy Spirit with great responsibilities.*
   b. *His falling away (v. 18-19)*
   c. *His impossibility to be restored back (he was killed: v. 21-24)*

Note: V. 4-8 is referring to saved people who have matured enough to be entrusted with leadership positions and responsibilities (see 5:14; 6:1) and have gotten into open sin and God removes them from that particular service with the warning that it is impossible to return to that position of `service again. ***It is not a matter of forgiveness; it is a matter of reaping what you sow.***

9 *But, beloved, we are persuaded better things of you, and things that accompany salvation, though we thus speak.*

II.   Heb. 10:26-31

When God Brings Chastisement
upon His Children

26 For if <u>we</u> sin wilfully after that <u>we</u> have received the knowledge of the truth, there remaineth no more sacrifice for sins,

Note: With the pronouns 'we', this passage is talking to believers.

Note: The only two possible different cases of sinning are to sin willfully in this case or sinning ignorantly. The sin here is doing wrong willfully despite knowing or having been taught better. Note the phrase "have received the knowledge of the truth". This is also called doing despite unto the Spirit of Grace. (v. 29)

Note: "No more sacrifice for sin" is referring to having no forgiveness for the act of sin and is not referring to forgiveness for the penalty of sin. The act of sinning ignorantly was covered until the sin was realized, but the act of sinning willfully required confession to restore fellowship with God or otherwise chastisement from God would come.

27 But a certain fearful looking for of judgment and fiery indignation, which shall devour the adversaries.

Note: "adversaries" [5227][2 times][contrary-Col. 2:14]

Note: The judgment is chastisement for Christians in whom God purges the contrary characteristics from

our lives. See Heb. 12:5-11 Verse 10 "that we might be partakers of his holiness"; Verse 11 "it yieldeth the peaceable fruit of righteousness unto them which are exercised thereby".

28 He that despised Moses' law died without mercy under two or three witnesses:

Note: "despised" (#114)(16x)(despise 8; reject 4; bring to nothing; frustrate; disannul; cast off)
Note: Disobeying God's commands after we are taught better is doing despite unto the Spirit of grace.

29 Of how much <u>sorer</u> punishment, suppose ye, shall he be thought worthy, who hath trodden under foot the Son of God, and hath counted the blood of the covenant, wherewith <u>he was sanctified</u>, an unholy thing, and hath done despite unto the Spirit of grace?

Note: "sorer" [5501][11 times][worse-10; sorer-1]
Note: The punishment is chastisement.
*Note: "he was sanctified" tells us the passage is referring to Christians. **Disobeying God's commands after we are taught better is doing despite unto the Spirit of grace and inviting God's chastening hand.***

30 For we know him that hath said, Vengeance [belongeth] unto me, I will <u>recompense</u>, saith the Lord. And again, <u>The Lord shall judge his people</u>.

Note: "recompense" (#467)(7x)(recompense 4; recompense again; repay; render)

Note: "The Lord shall judge his people" is referring to Christians being chastised by God. See Heb. 12:5-11

Note: "Vengeance belongs to God" [See Deut. 32:35; Psa. 94:1; Rom. 12:19]

31 [It is] a fearful thing to fall into the hands of the living God.

Note: No one comes back from God's woodshed of chastisement laughing or mocking or joking.

III. James 2:14-26

Vain Faith versus True Faith
You can Hear Vain Faith but you Can't See it Work

14 What [doth it] <u>profit</u>, my brethren, though a man **say** he hath faith, and have not works? can faith save him?

Note: "profit" [3786][3 times][def. benefit]
Note: The faith that cannot produce works cannot produce salvation.

Vain Faith Just Talks

15 If a brother or sister be naked, and destitute of daily food,

16 And one of you **say** unto them, Depart in peace, be [ye] warmed and filled; notwithstanding ye give them not those things which are needful to the body; what [doth it] profit?

Note: See the use of the word "say". The faith that only talks, is a vain faith, and only deceives people into thinking they are saved.

Vain Faith gets no Results

17 Even so faith, if it hath not works, is dead, being alone.

Note: True faith changes more than your talk. It also changes your way of life.

Man Sees Our Faith Through our Works

18 Yea, a man may say, Thou hast faith, and I have works: shew me thy faith without thy works, and I will shew thee my faith by my works.

Note: The only way we can see a person's faith is through their works.

Vain Faith is Vague

19 Thou believest that there is one God; thou doest well: the devils also believe, and tremble.

Note: It does not say here that the devils believe the Gospel of Jesus Christ, but just that they believe there is one God. Just because you are not an atheist does not mean that you are saved or born again.

20 But wilt thou know, O vain man, that faith without works is dead?

Note: ["vain faith" I Cor. 15:2, 14]

Example of Real Faith (In Abraham)

21 Was not Abraham our father justified by works, when he had offered Isaac his son upon the altar?

Note: [see Romans 4:2] [This is outward justification in the sight of man.][See Rom. 2:13 - outward justification]

22 Seest thou how faith wrought with his works, and by works was faith made perfect ?

23 And the scripture was fulfilled which saith, Abraham believed God, and it was imputed unto him for righteousness: and he was called the Friend of God.

Note: C.R. Gen. 15:6
Note: "Friend of God" II Chron. 20:7; Isai. 41:8

Outward Justification

24 Ye see then how that by works a man is justified, and not by faith only.

Note: [this is outward justification in the sight of man]

Example of Real Faith (In Rahab)

25 Likewise also was not Rahab the harlot justified by works, when she had received the messengers, and had sent [them] out another way?

Vain Faith Compared to a Dead Body
(BOTH ARE LEFT EMPTY)

26 For as the body without the spirit is dead, so faith without works is dead also.

Note: Titus 1:16 "They profess that they know God; but in works they deny him, being abominable, and disobedient, and unto every good work reprobate."

Note: Faith alone saves alone, but the faith that saves is not alone.

*Note: **True faith produces salvation and true faith produces works but works can never produce salvation.***

IV.   Gal. 5:4

Fallen from Grace's Reach not
Fallen from Salvation

4 Christ is become of no effect unto you, whosoever of you are justified by the law; ye are fallen <1601> from grace.

Note: "fallen" [1601][14x][fall-7; fall off-2; hath taken none effect; be cast; faileth; fallen; fall away]

*Note: **The people Paul is referring to here he refers to throughout this book. They are lost people that are attempting to be justified by the works of the law.***

Gal. 1:7 "...but there be some that trouble you, and would pervert the gospel of Christ."

Gal. 2:4 "And that because of false brethren unawares brought in, who came in privily to spy out our liberty which we have in Christ Jesus, that they might bring us into bondage:"

Gal. 2:6 "But of these who seemed to be somewhat, (whatsoever they were, it maketh no matter to me: God accepteth no man's person:) for they who seemed [to be somewhat] in conference added nothing to me:"

Gal. 4:17 "They zealously affect you, [but] not well; yea, they would exclude you, that ye might affect them."

Gal. 5:10 "...: but he that troubleth you shall bear his judgment, whosoever he be."

Gal. 5:12 "I would they were even cut off which trouble you."

Gal. 6:12 "As many as desire to make a fair shew in the flesh, they constrain you to be circumcised; only lest they should suffer persecution for the cross of Christ."

Gal. 6:13 "For neither they themselves who are circumcised keep the law; but desire to have you circumcised, that they may glory in your flesh."

Note: These people are lost people who insist upon being saved by keeping the law and working or good deeding their way to heaven.

Note: The Bible makes it very plain that it is impossible to be saved by works:[Eph. 2:8-9; Gal. 2:16; Titus 3:5-7; Rom. 3:20, 28; 4:5] "ye are fallen from grace" is referring to these lost people who insist upon being saved by works that they do. They have fallen from the grace that brings salvation. It is important to note that these lost people fell from grace, not from salvation. Grace is not salvation but it is access to salvation. Because of insisting upon being saved by works they have callused themselves from believing that salvation is through faith in Christ and are fallen from the grace that brings salvation. **Tit 2:11** *For the grace of God that bringeth salvation hath appeared to all men,*

"Christ is become of no effect unto you" means they have crossed one of God's deadlines and are no longer able to be saved.

Mat 7:21 Not every one that saith unto me, Lord, Lord, shall enter into the kingdom of heaven; but he that doeth the will of my Father which is in heaven.

Mat 7:22 Many will say to me in that day, <u>Lord, Lord, have we not prophesied in thy name and in thy name have cast out devils? and in thy name done many wonderful works?</u>

Mat 7:23 And then will I profess unto them, I never knew you: depart from me, ye that work iniquity.

The above passage shows us people who were so sure that works saved them that they argued with God at the White Throne Judgment on Judgment Day. They presented their works as a defense thinking it would get them into heaven.

V.   Luke 9:62

Luke 9:62 And Jesus said unto him, No man, having put his hand to the plough, and looking back, is fit for the kingdom of God.

[The phrase "kingdom of God" appears 69 times in the bible and are all in the N.T. Not every place does "kingdom of God" refer to the third heaven. In some it does not.][See Luke 13:18-21]
Note: These parables 'The grain of mustard seed'; 'The leaven and 3 measure of meal' (seen also in Matt. 13:31-33) are referring to the ministry down here on Earth, not up in heaven. Especially note the "leaven" is down here on earth and not up in heaven.
[See also Luke 10:9-11; 11:20]

The "kingdom of God" in Luke 9:62 is referring to the ministry and work of God down here on earth and not the third heaven and final home of the believer.

Note: "Put his hand to the plough" is referring to the child of God starting some kind of service in the ministry for God. "Looking back" is referring to the child of God having second thoughts about the service or regretting leaving something for the service.
"fit for the kingdom of God" [fit # 2111 - 3 times; Luke 14:35 "fit"; Heb. 6:7 "meet"; and here] ***The individual is not fit for service in the kingdom of heaven down here due to his heart being elsewhere.****[See II Tim. 4:10 about "Demas"]*

37

VI.   Rev. 22:14

Getting Saved is a Command From God

14 Blessed [are] they that do his commandments, that they may have right <1849> to the tree of life, and may enter in through the gates into the city.

Note: "right" [1849][103 times][authority; power; jurisdiction; liberty; strength]
Note: [See Gal. 2:16, 21; 3:11, 21, 24; Eph. 2:8-9; Titus 3:5-7; Rom. 3:20, 28; 4:5; 5:18-19] It is impossible to keep all of God's commands. If keeping all of God's commands is required for salvation, no one will be saved. Keeping God's commands cannot save you but doing the commandments of repenting and believing the gospel does save you.
Note: "tree of life" [Gen. 2:9; 3:22, 24; Prov. 3:18; 11:30; 13:12; 15:4][Rev. 2:7; 22:2; 22:14] In Rev. 2:7 "To him that overcometh will I give to eat of the tree of life, which is in the midst of the paradise of God."
Note: We overcome by trusting Christ as our Savior. I John 5:4 "For whatsoever is born of God overcometh the world: and this is the victory that overcometh the world, even our faith." I John 5:5 "Who is he that overcometh the world, but he that believeth that Jesus is the Son of God?"
Note: We gain access to the tree of life by overcoming or trusting Christ as Savior.
Note: The commands referred to in Rev. 22:14 are commands to get saved. Mark 1:15 "repent ye, and believe the gospel" II Pet. 2:21 "For it had been better

*for them not to have known the way of righteousness,
than, after they have known it, to turn from the holy
commandment delivered unto them." John 3:7 "Ye
must be born again" Acts 17:30 "And the times of this
ignorance God winked at; but now commandeth all
men ever where to repent:" I John 3:23 "this is his
commandment, That we should believe on the name of
his Son Jesus Christ, and love one another, as he gave
us commandment." Note: Getting saved is not a request
from God. It is a command of God.*

VII. Heb. 12:14

Hebrews 12:14 Follow peace with all *men*, and <u>holiness,
without which no man shall see the Lord:</u>

*Note: #38 holiness 5, sanctification 5 (10 times)
Rom 6:19; Rom 6:22; 1Co 1:30; 1Th 4:3-4; 1Th 4:7; 2Th
2:13; 1Ti 2:15;Heb 12:14; 1Pe 1:2*
*Note: The holiness that is mentioned in this verse is
not our holiness or our righteousness. It is a reference
to God's holiness or righteousness.*

Isaiah 64:6 But we are all as an unclean *thing*, and <u>all
our righteousnesses *are* as filthy rags</u>; and we all do
fade as a leaf; and our iniquities, like the wind, have
taken us away.

Matthew 5:20 For I say unto you, That except your
righteousness shall exceed *the righteousness* of the

scribes and Pharisees, ye shall in no case enter into the kingdom of heaven.

Note: The point of the above verses is that all our own righteousness is not good enough to get us to God and heaven. We must have the holiness and righteousness of God imputed unto us. There is only one way to do this.

Romans 3:22 Even the righteousness of God *which is* by faith of Jesus Christ unto all and upon all them that believe: for there is no difference:

When we trust Christ as our personal Savior we receive the righteousness of Jesus Christ which is the only righteousness that is good enough for getting us to God. The people who are depending on their own holiness or righteousness for their salvation might as well be depending on filthy rags (Isaiah 64:6) for their salvation.

VIII. Philippians 2:12

12 Wherefore, my beloved, as ye have always obeyed, not as in my presence only, but now much more in my absence, <u>work out your own salvation</u> with fear and trembling.

Note: To work out your own salvation is to work out what God has already worked in according to verse **13. "For it is God which worketh in you both to will and to do of his good pleasure**.*" It says "work out"* *not (work for) your own salvation. This verse is not suggesting that you can work for your salvation. Note the following verses.*

Ephesians 2:8 For by grace are ye saved through faith; and that not of yourselves: *it is* the gift of God: **9** Not of works, lest any man should boast.

Titus 3:5 Not by works of righteousness which we have done, but according to his mercy he saved us, by the washing of regeneration, and renewing of the Holy Ghost;

Galatians 2:16 Knowing that a man is not justified by the works of the law, but by the faith of Jesus Christ, even we have believed in Jesus Christ, that we might be justified by the faith of Christ, and not by the works of the law: for by the works of the law shall no flesh be justified.

Romans 5:18-19 Therefore as by the offence of one *judgment came* upon all men to condemnation; even so by the righteousness of one *the free gift came* upon all men unto justification of life. 19 For as by one man's disobedience many were made sinners, so by the obedience of one shall many be made righteous.

*Note: Consider how Jesus said it which explains the point of **Phil. 2:12**.*

Matthew 5:16 Let your light so shine before men, that they may see your good works, and glorify your Father which is in heaven.

IX. I Corinthians 6:9-11 and Gal. 5:19-21 and Eph. 5:5-8

(The reason for listing these three passages together is because the explanation for all three is basically the same.)

I Corinthians 6:9 Know ye not that the unrighteous shall not inherit the kingdom of God? Be not deceived: neither fornicators, nor idolaters, nor adulterers, nor effeminate, nor abusers of themselves with mankind,

10 Nor thieves, nor covetous, nor drunkards, nor revilers, nor extortioners, shall inherit the kingdom of God.

11 And such **were** some of you: but ye are washed, but ye are sanctified, but ye are justified in the name of the Lord Jesus, and by the Spirit of our God.

Note: The people who would try to use this passage to impose works into the plan of salvation, seem to anxiously use verse 9 and 10 and leave out verse 11. What the passage is saying is that the person who can freely practice these sins[fornication; idolatry; adultery; or homosexuality; steeling; covetousness; drunkards; reviling; extortions]or any sins is lost. If there is no chastening from God as taught in Heb. 12:5-11 to stop them from practicing sin, they are lost. Note the following:

Note: Many things will stop a Christian from freely practicing sin:

A. *A divine nature with divine desires (II Pet. 1:4) [wanting to obey God and not wanting to disobey God]*
B. *Chastisement from God (Heb. 12:5-11)*
C. *The indwelling of the Holy Spirit (Eph. 1:13; Gal. 3:2, 14)*
    [bringing progressive change in our lives](II Cor. 5:17)
D. *A purged conscience. (Heb. 9:14)*
E. *A new heart in which to love (Ez. 11:19; 36:26) [loving God and Christians and not loving the pride and lust of the world]*
F. *Because of a threefold promise from God to every believer:*
    1) *"every branch that beareth fruit, he purgeth it, that it may bring forth more fruit." (John 15:2)*
    2) *"For whom he did foreknow, he also did predestinate to be conformed to the image of his Son" (Rom. 8:29)*
    3) *"Being confident of this very thing, that he which hath begun a good work in you will perform it until the day of Jesus Christ:" (Phil. 1:6)*
G. *Premature death. (I John 5:16)*

Now a look at verse 11: And such were some of you: but ye are washed, but ye are sanctified, but ye

43

*are justified in the name of the Lord Jesus, and by the Spirit of our God. What God does for us at salvation takes us from freely practicing sin to when we sin we are promised chastisement from God. Verse 11 makes it clear that we were freely practicing sin (such **were** some of you) but we are washed, sanctified, and justified in the name of the Lord Jesus and by the Spirit.*

Note the following examples:

1) *King David committed murder and adultery and was greatly chastised of God for his sins. II Sam. 12:7-12 **(B. Chastisement from God (Heb. 12:5-11))***
2) *King Saul died a premature death for his wickedness: I Chron. 10:13-14*

Samuel states that Saul went to be with him in paradise.

*1 Samuel 28:19 Moreover the LORD will also deliver Israel with thee into the hand of the Philistines: and tomorrow shalt thou and thy sons be with me: the LORD also shall deliver the host of Israel into the hand of the Philistines. **(G. Premature death. (I John 5:16))***

Galatians 5:19-21

19 Now the works of the flesh are manifest, which are these; Adultery, fornication, uncleanness, lasciviousness,

20 Idolatry, witchcraft, hatred, variance, emulations, wrath, strife, seditions, heresies,

*21 Envyings, murders, drunkenness, revellings, and such like: of the which I tell you before, as I have also told you in time past, <u>that they which **do** such things shall not inherit the kingdom of God.</u>*

Note: the verb "do" is in the present tense which speaks of continuous action. The same explanation fits here as was for I Cor. 6:9-11. If a person can freely practice these sins or any sins without the chastening hand of God, they are lost.

Ephesians 5:5-8

5 For this ye know, that no <u>whoremonger</u>, nor <u>unclean person</u>, nor <u>covetous man</u>, who is an <u>idolater</u>, hath any inheritance in the kingdom of Christ and of God.

6 Let no man deceive you with vain words: for because of these things cometh the wrath of God upon the children of disobedience.

7 Be not ye therefore partakers with them.

*8 <u>For ye **were** sometimes darkness, but now are ye light in the Lord: walk as children of light:</u>*

Note: This passage like the other two has the same explanation. Verse 8 says they were sometimes darkness, but now are ye light in the Lord. To restate the point, any person that can freely practice these sins without the chastisement of God is lost.

In the book of I John the explanation between act of sin and freely practicing sin is explained in more detail. Note the following:

*1 **John** 1:8 If we say that we have no sin, we deceive ourselves, and the truth is not in us.*

*1 **John** 1:10 If we say that we have not sinned, we make him a liar, and his word is not in us.*

Note: These verses make it clear that we have all sinned but notice the next verses.

*1 **John** 3:8-9 He that committeth sin is of the devil; for the devil sinneth from the beginning. For this purpose the Son of God was manifested, that he might destroy the works of the devil.*

9 Whosoever is born of God doth not commit sin; for his seed remaineth in him: and he cannot sin, because he is born of God.

Note: Comparing the two sets of scripture it would appear that not only have we all sinned but it seems that no one will be able to be saved and go to heaven. But looking closely at the passages, the second passage is referring to freely practicing sin. The verbs, "committeth" and "commit" are the present tense which is continuous action. Verse 9 even gives us one of the reasons that a Christian cannot freely practice sin. He has been given divine seed inside of him at his spiritual birth that stops him from freely practicing sin.

X.   Revelation 21:8

But the fearful, and unbelieving, and the abominable, and murderers, and whoremongers, and sorcerers, and idolaters, and all liars, shall have <u>their part</u> in the lake which burneth with fire and brimstone: which is the second death.

Note: Unbelievers are mentioned separately and some would think that this would imply that the others are believers but sinful. First looking at "unbelief" notice the following passages:

John 3:18 He that believeth on him is not condemned: but **he that believeth not** is condemned already, because he hath not believed in the name of the only begotten Son of God.

John 3:36 He that believeth on the Son hath everlasting life: and **he that believeth not** the Son shall not see life; but the wrath of God abideth on him.

John 16:8-11 And when he is come, he will reprove the world of sin, and of righteousness, and of judgment:

9 Of **sin, because they believe not on me**;

10 Of righteousness, because I go to my Father, and ye see me no more;

11 Of judgment, because the prince of this world is judged.

Note: It is the sin of unbelief that takes a man to Hell. The passage in Revelation 21:8 is referring to the sentence of the unbelievers at the White Throne Judgment. They are all unbelievers but some are unbelieving murderers, some unbelieving liars, some unbelieving whoremongers and so on. They are sentenced to their part in the lake of fire. Without taking up too much space on this subject in this book, the Bible does teach different degrees of punishment in the lake of fire. See the following references: Deut. 32:22; Psa. 86:13; Prov. 9:18; Matt. 23:14-15; Mark 12:40; Luke 20:47

XI. Romans 2:7-10 Eternal Rewards for the Saved

7 To them who by patient continuance in well doing seek for glory and honour and immortality, eternal life:

Note: Here eternal life is not referring to salvation, in many other places it does. [Example] John 3:15-16, 36; 5:24; 6:40, 47; 10:28; Rom. 6:23; I Tim. 1:16; I John 2:25; 5:13 all refer to salvation.

1) *Jesus is called eternal life. (I John 1:2)(For the life was manifested, and we have seen it, and bear witness, and shew unto you that eternal life, which was with the Father, and was manifested unto us;) (1 John 5:20) (And we know that the Son of God is come, and hath given us an understanding, that we may know him that*

48

is true, and we are in him that is true, [even] in
his Son Jesus Christ. This is the true God, and
eternal life.)

2) *The bible is called eternal life. (John 12:50)(And
I know that his commandment is life everlasting:
whatsoever I speak therefore, even as the Father
said unto me, so I speak.) (1 John 5:11)(And this
is the record, that God hath given to us eternal
life, and this life is in his Son.)*

3) *Our rewards in heaven are called eternal
life. (John 4:36)(And he that reapeth receiveth
wages, and gathereth fruit unto life eternal: that
both he that soweth and he that reapeth may
rejoice together.) (John 6:27)(Labour not for the
meat which perisheth, but for that meat which
endureth unto everlasting life, which the Son of
man shall give unto you: for him hath God the
Father sealed.)*

*Note: Eternal life in 'Rom. 2:7' is referring to
eternal rewards for the true believer who "by patient
continuance in well doing seek for glory and honour
and immorality."*

Eternal Damnation for the Lost

8 But unto them that are contentious, and do not obey
the truth, but obey unrighteousness, indignation and
wrath,

9 Tribulation and anguish, upon every soul of man that
doeth evil, of the Jew first, and also of the Gentile;

Note: v. 8-9 are referring to eternal degrees of punishment to the unbelievers who "are contentious, and do not obey the truth, but obey unrighteousness" they are promised "indignation and wrath, tribulation and anguish, upon every soul of man that doeth evil"

Note: v. 7-9 are 'judgement verses' not 'salvation verses' (see v. 5, 6 & 10)

Eternal Rewards to the Saved

10 But glory, honour, and peace, to every man that worketh good, to the Jew first, and also to the Gentile:

Note: This verse is talking to saved people. We cannot expect lost people to work good.

XII. Hebrew 3:6 and 3:14 Genuine Faith Is Not Temporary

Hebrews 3:6 But Christ as a son over his own house; whose house are we, if we hold fast the confidence and the rejoicing of the hope firm unto the end.

Hebrews 3:14 For we are made partakers of Christ, if we hold the beginning of our confidence stedfast unto the end;

Note: If a person is genuinely saved, as a result, they will "hold the beginning of their confidence steadfast unto the end." Genuine faith brings genuine salvation. A true test of genuine salvation is how our faith lasts through time. If it is a temporary belief, it *is not a genuine faith. It is a mere consideration. <u>The following verses prove this point.</u>*

Heb. 10:38 *Now the just shall live by faith: but if [any man] draw back, my soul shall have no pleasure in him.*

39 But we are not of them who draw back unto perdition; but of them that believe to the saving of the soul.

1 John 2:19 *They went out from us, but they were not of us; for if they had been of us, they would [no doubt] have continued with us: but [they went out],that they might be made manifest that they were not all of us.*

Temporary Faith or Mere Consideration versus Genuine Faith

Luke 8:13 *They on the rock are they, which, when they hear, receive the word with joy; and these have no root, <u>which for a while believe</u>, and in time of temptation fall away.*

John 3:15-16 *That whosoever **believeth** in him should not perish, but have eternal life. 16 For God so loved the world, that he gave his only begotten on, that whosoever **believeth** in him should not perish, but have everlasting life.*

*Note: The verbs "believeth" #4100 (248x)(believe 239, commit unto 4, <u>commit to (one's) trust</u> 1, be committed unto 1, be put in trust with 1, <u>be commit to one's trust</u> 1, believer 1) Verb #5723 tense: **present tense** which is **continuous***

Note: The continuous faith does not mean that salvation is progressive or that you depend on your faith to get you to heaven. The person that is persuaded that Jesus and what He did for him on the cross is what he is depending on to get him to heaven has continuous faith.

XIII. I Corinthians 15:1-2

1 Corinthians 15:1-2 Moreover, brethren, I declare unto you the gospel which I preached unto you, which also ye have received, and wherein ye stand; By which also ye are saved, **if** ye keep in memory what I preached unto you, <u>unless ye have **believed in vain**</u>.

Note: The "believed in vain" is further discussed in the same chapter. Verse 14 and verse 17.

1 Corinthians 15:14 And if Christ be not risen, then *is* our preaching vain, and <u>your faith *is* also vain.</u>

1 Corinthians 15:17 And if Christ be not raised, <u>your faith *is* vain</u>; ye are yet in your sins.

Romans 10:9 That if thou shalt confess with thy mouth the Lord Jesus, and <u>shalt believe in thine heart that God hath raised him from the dead, thou shalt be saved.</u>

1 John 5:1 <u>Whosoever believeth that Jesus is the Christ is born of God</u>: and every one that loveth him that begat loveth him also that is begotten of him.

What would make their faith vain is to not believe the proper facts about Jesus first before you can trust Christ as Savior. Example: Some believed in Jesus but did not believe in His Resurrection. Some believe in Jesus but not that He is God the Son. Some believe in Jesus but believe that Jesus was a created being. Some believe in Jesus but are depending on their life style to get them to heaven instead of Jesus. Some believe in Jesus but want to make Jesus Lord of their life before they trust Jesus first as their Savior. All these have believed in vain. It is just as important to believe who Jesus is as it is to believe in and trust Jesus as your Savior.

XIV. Matthew 5:20

Matthew 5:20 For I say unto you, That except your righteousness shall exceed *the righteousness* of the scribes and Pharisees, ye shall in no case enter into the kingdom of heaven.

*Note: The only way our righteousness can exceed the righteousness of the scribes and Pharisees is to trust Christ as Savior and receive His righteousness. Note the following verses: **Romans 3:21-22** But now the righteousness of God without the law is manifested, being witnessed by the law and the prophets; **22** Even the righteousness of God which is by faith of Jesus Christ unto all and upon all them that believe: for there is no difference:*

XV.   II Peter 2:20-22

Delusion with Reform Instead of
Deliverance by Regeneration

20 For if after they have escaped the pollutions of the world <u>through the knowledge of the Lord and Saviour Jesus Christ</u>, they are again entangled therein, and overcome, the latter end is worse with them than the beginning.

Note: It says 'they have escaped ... through the knowledge of the Lord not through the salvation of the Lord and Savior Jesus Christ.
Note: Many people are trying to reform to the commands and life style that Jesus taught instead of trusting Christ as Savior and letting God change them.

21 For it had been better for them not to have known the way of righteousness, than, after they have known [it], to turn from the holy commandment delivered unto them.

Note: It was said of Judas Iscariot "good were it for that man if he had never been born" Mark 14:21
Note: The holy command that is rejected is "repent and believe the gospel". [Acts 17:30; Mk. 1:15]

22 But it is happened unto them according to the true proverb, The dog [is] turned to his own vomit again; and the sow that was washed to her wallowing in the mire.

Note: "proverb" [3942][5 times][4 times 'proverb'; 1 time 'parable']

Note: In reformation the dog is still a dog and the pig is still a pig and both are only temporarily cleaned up and so still want to go back to their old filth. In regeneration the individual becomes a new creature and is no longer a dog or a pig and has a holy desire to go God's way.

Note: 2 Cor. 5:17 Therefore if any man [be] in Christ, [he is] a new creature: old things are passed away; behold, all things are become new.

Note: Consider the following as an example:

Matt. 12:43 *When the unclean spirit is gone out of a man, he walketh through dry places, seeking rest, and findeth none. 44 Then he saith, I will return into my house from whenceI came out; and when he is come, he findeth [it] **empty,** swept, and garnished. 45 Then goeth he, and taketh with himself seven other spirits more wicked than himself, and they enter in and dwell there: and the last [state] of that man is worse than the first. Even so shall it be also unto this wicked generation.*

Note: Reform only brings temporary change, and leaves the individual empty and makes matters worse. Regeneration by trusting Christ as Savior brings real salvation and real change.

Note: Reform also gives a person false security and a maybe type hope of heaven.

XVI. Luke 15:11-32

11 And he said, A certain man had two sons:

12 And the younger of them said to *his* father, Father, give me the portion of goods that falleth *to me*. And he divided unto them *his* living.

13 And not many days after the younger son gathered all together, and took his journey into a far country, and there wasted his substance with riotous living.

14 And when he had spent all, there arose a mighty famine in that land; and he began to be in want.

15 And he went and joined himself to a citizen of that country; and he sent him into his fields to feed swine.

16 And he would fain have filled his belly with the husks that the swine did eat: and no man gave unto him.

17 And <u>when he came to himself,</u> he said, How many hired servants of **<u>my father's</u>** have bread enough and to spare, and I perish with hunger!

Note: "when he came to himself" This is not picturing an unbeliever getting saved. It is picturing a saved person getting his heart right again with God. The unbeliever comes to Jesus for salvation. The backslider comes to himself, remembering who he is and the mistakes that he made. At no time in this story was the son not the son of the father. Even in his backslidden condition here he addresses his father as "my father".

18 I will arise and go to **my father**, and will say unto him, **Father**, I have sinned against heaven, and before thee,

19 And am <u>no more worthy to be called thy son</u>: make me as one of thy hired servants.

Note: He was not worthy but he was still his son.

20 And he arose, and came to <u>his father</u>. But when he was yet a great way off, <u>his father</u> saw him, and had compassion, and ran, and fell on his neck, and kissed him.

21 And <u>the son</u> said unto him, Father, I have sinned against heaven, and in thy sight, and am <u>no more worthy to be called thy son.</u>

22 But the <u>father</u> said to his servants, Bring forth the best robe, and put *it* on him; and put a ring on his hand, and shoes on *his* feet:

23 And bring hither the fatted calf, and kill *it*; and let us eat, and be merry:

24 For this <u>my son</u> was <u>dead, and is alive again; he was lost, and is found</u>. And they began to be merry.

Note: "was dead and is alive again" "was lost and is found"
*Note: The term "dead" is not a reference to an unbeliever. It is a reference to a believer who yielded to the lust of the flesh. **Romans 6:12-13** Let not sin therefore reign in your mortal body, that ye should*

obey it in the lusts thereof. **13** *Neither yield ye your members as instruments of unrighteousness unto sin: but yield yourselves unto God, as <u>those that are **alive from the dead**</u>, and your members as instruments of righteousness unto God.*

Note: The term "lost" is not a reference to an unbeliever. It is a reference to a believer who lost his testimony and effectiveness for Christ.

Matthew 5:13 *Ye are the salt of the earth: but if the salt have <u>**lost his savour**</u>, wherewith shall it be salted? it is thenceforth good for nothing, but to be cast out, and to be trodden under foot of men.*

Mark 9:50 *Salt is good: but if the salt <u>**have lost his saltness**</u>, wherewith will ye season it? Have salt in yourselves, and have peace one with another.*

Note: The backslider regained his fellowship back with his Father. When the father made the comment about "was dead and is alive again" "was lost and is found" he was not saying he was his son, then not his son, and then is his son again. That would be ridiculous.

25 Now his elder son was in the field: and as he came and drew nigh to the house, he heard musick and dancing.

26 And he called one of the servants, and asked what these things meant.

27 And he said unto him, Thy brother is come; and thy father hath killed the fatted calf, because he hath received him safe and sound.

28 And he was angry, and would not go in: therefore came his father out, and intreated him.

29 And he answering said to *his* father, Lo, these many years do I serve thee, neither transgressed I at any time thy commandment: and yet thou never gavest me a kid, that I might make merry with my friends:

30 But as soon as this <u>thy son</u> was come, which hath devoured thy living with harlots, thou hast killed for him the fatted calf.

31 And he said unto him, Son, thou art ever with me, and all that I have is thine.

32 It was meet that we should make merry, and be glad: for this thy brother <u>was dead, and is alive again; and was lost, and is found.</u>

Note: "was dead and is alive again...was lost and is found" (See notes at verse 24.)

Note: Comparing this parable with the previous two parables and note the differences. In the parable of the lost sheep and lost silver there was a diligent search and a closing remark about rejoicing in heaven over one sinner that repents. In the parable of the prodigal son there was no search at all nor a comment about the rejoicing in heaven over one sinner that repents. There is a reason for this. The prodigal son is not picturing an unbeliever becoming a believer. It is picturing a backslidden believer coming back in fellowship with his heavenly Father.

XVII. Luke 12:41-48 (Matthew 24:45-51)

Luke 12:41- 48 Then Peter said unto him, Lord, speakest thou this parable unto __us__, or even __to all__?

Note: The question Peter asked is the key to the explanation of these verses. By our Lord's answer the parable is __to all__. So the application is not to just believers (as in "us") but also to unbelievers (as in "to all"). The total human population is spoken about. He speaks to the faithful and wise servants as well as to the abusive and evil servants. All servants both saved and lost are the ones Jesus speaks about.

First the Servant that is Saved

42 And the Lord said, Who then is <u>that faithful and wise steward</u>, whom his lord shall make ruler over his household, to give them their portion of meat in due season?

43 Blessed <u>is that servant</u>, whom his lord when he cometh shall find so doing.

44 Of a truth I say unto you, that <u>he will make him ruler over all that he hath</u>.

Now the Servant that is Lost

45 But and <u>if that servant</u> say in his heart, My lord delayeth his coming; and shall begin to beat the menservants and maidens, and to eat and drink, and to be drunken;

Note: "if that servant" **Matt. 24:48** *says "if that evil servant"*

46 *The lord of* <u>that servant</u> *will come in a day when he looketh not for him, and at an hour when he is not aware, and* <u>will cut him in sunder, and will appoint him his portion with the unbelievers.</u>

Note: "his portion with the unbelievers" **Matt. 24:51** *says "his portion with the hypocrites" Being with the hypocrites he was pretending to be saved. The reason for him being given his portion with the unbelievers is because he is an unbeliever.*

47 <u>*And that servant, which knew his lord's will, and prepared not himself, neither did according to his will, shall be beaten with many stripes*</u>*.*

Note: The lost servant that knows how to be saved and refuses or does not prepare himself shall be judged worse in the Lake of Fire than the lost servant that knew not.

Note: **John 6:40** *And* <u>**this is the will of him that sent me**</u><u>*, that every one which seeth the Son, and believeth on him, may have everlasting life*</u>*: and I will raise him up at the last day.*

48 <u>*But he that knew not, and did commit things worthy of stripes, shall be beaten with few stripes.*</u> *For unto whomsoever much is given, of him shall be much required: and to whom men have committed much, of him they will ask the more.*

Note: **Matt. 24:51** *concludes with "there shall be weeping and gnashing of teeth".*

Note: So the parable reminds us of the two final judgments. For the lost it is the White Throne Judgment and then their part in the lake of fire and for the saved it is the Judgment Seat of Christ and their rewards in heaven.

The Saved Servant

Matthew 24:45-51 *Who then <u>is a faithful and wise servant</u>, whom his lord hath made ruler over his household, to give them meat in due season?*

46 *Blessed is that servant, whom his lord when he cometh shall find so doing.*

47 *Verily I say unto you, That he shall make him ruler over all his goods.*

The Lost Servant

48 *But <u>and if that evil servant</u> shall say in his heart, My lord delayeth his coming;*

49 *And shall begin to smite his fellowservants, and to eat and drink with the drunken;*

50 *The lord of that servant shall come in a day when he looketh not for him, and in an hour that he is not aware of,*

51 And <u>shall cut him asunder, and appoint him his portion with the hypocrites: there shall be weeping and gnashing of teeth.</u>

XVIII. Matthew 25:1-13

Ten Virgins (Five Wise and Five Foolish)

1 Then shall the kingdom of heaven be likened unto ten virgins, which took their lamps, and went forth to meet the bridegroom.

2 And five of them were wise, and five were foolish.

*3 They that were foolish took their lamps, **and took no oil with them**:*

*4 But **the wise took oil** in their vessels with their lamps.*

5 While the bridegroom tarried, they all slumbered and slept.

6 And at midnight there was a cry made, Behold, the bridegroom cometh; go ye out to meet him.

7 Then all those virgins arose, and trimmed their lamps.

8 And the foolish said unto the wise, Give us of your oil; for our lamps are gone out.

9 But the wise answered, saying, Not so; lest there be not enough for us and you: but go ye rather to them that sell, and buy for yourselves.

10 And while they went to buy, the bridegroom came; and they that were ready went in with him to the marriage: and the door was shut.

11 Afterward came also the other virgins, saying, Lord, Lord, open to us.

12 But he answered and said, Verily I say unto you, I know you not.

13 Watch therefore, for ye know neither the day nor the hour wherein the Son of man cometh.

Note: Things in common:

1) *All ten were virgins (representing their morally religious life style)*
2) *All ten had lamps (representing each ones testimony)*
3) *All ten looked for the bridegroom (representing the universal awareness of the second coming)*
4) *All ten slumbered and slept (representing poor alertness of them all)*
   (A slumbering Christian can look very similar to a religious lost person)
5) *All ten arose and trimmed their lamps (representing human effort in getting ready)*

Note: Things that are different:

1) *Five were wise and five were foolish (The wise took care of something important in their lives that the foolish did not)*

2) *The foolish took no oil with them but the wise took oil in their vessels*
   (The difference is the oil)(representing the Holy Spirit)
3) *The foolish virgins' lamps went out but the wise virgins' lamps did not.*
   Proverbs 13:9 *The light of the righteous rejoiceth: but the lamp of the wicked shall be put out.*
4) *The wise were ready but the foolish were not*
5) *The wise went with the bridegroom and the foolish were left behind*

Note: This parable shows that the lost can do a lot of things that the saved can do but acting like a Christian does not make you a Christian. The oil or the spiritual birth makes the difference. You cannot fake the spiritual birth. It must come from God.

John 3:6 *That which is born of the flesh is flesh; and* **_that which is born of the Spirit is spirit._**

Chapter 5

The Matter of those being Raised from the Dead

*Note: There are only one of two places a person can go after he dies and that is Heaven or Hell. This takes place instantly at death. The soul at death leaves the body and goes to Heaven or Hell. When these people are raised from the dead, they were not in Hell because that would give them another chance to be saved. They were pulled from paradise. **If it is possible in this life to lose your salvation,** bringing them back from the dead would give them another opportunity to lose their salvation. This would be a terrible thing to do to anyone who is in paradise.*

Note: Here are some different examples in the bible of those that were raised from the dead:

Raising the Young Maid

Matthew 9:18 While he spake these things unto them, behold, there came a certain ruler, and worshipped him, saying, <u>My daughter is even now dead</u>: but come and lay thy hand upon her, and she shall live. 19 And Jesus arose, and followed him, and *so did* his disciples. 23 And when Jesus came into the ruler's house, and saw the minstrels and the people making a noise, 24 He said unto them, Give place: <u>for the maid is not dead, but</u>

sleepeth. And they laughed him to scorn. 25 But when the people were put forth, he went in, <u>and took her by the hand, and the maid arose</u>.

Note: *So was the maid lost when she died? If she was she was in Hell. If she was in Hell, she was given a second chance out of Hell. No doubt she was saved and went to paradise. So if she was saved before she died and went to paradise and could lose her salvation, then when Jesus raised her from the dead he actually gave her another chance to be lost. This is a terrible thing to do to someone who was once in paradise.*

Mark 5:35 While he yet spake, there came from the ruler of the synagogue's *house certain* which said, <u>Thy daughter is dead</u>: why troublest thou the Master any further? 36 As soon as Jesus heard the word that was spoken, he saith unto the ruler of the synagogue, Be not afraid, only believe. 37 And he suffered no man to follow him, save Peter, and James, and John the brother of James. 38 And he cometh to the house of the ruler of the synagogue, and seeth the tumult, and them that wept and wailed greatly. 39 And when he was come in, he saith unto them, Why make ye this ado, and weep? <u>the damsel is not dead, but sleepeth.</u> 40 And they laughed him to scorn. But when he had put them all out, he taketh the father and the mother of the damsel, and them that were with him, and entereth in where the damsel was lying. 41 <u>And he took the damsel by the hand, and said unto her, Talitha cumi; which is, being interpreted, Damsel, I say unto thee, arise</u>. 42 And <u>straightway the damsel arose, and walked;</u> for she was *of the age of* twelve years. And they were astonished with a great astonishment. 43 And he charged them straitly that no man should know it; and commanded that something should be given her to eat.

Luke 8:49 While he yet spake, there cometh one from the ruler of the synagogue's *house*, saying to him, Thy daughter is dead; trouble not the Master. 50 But when Jesus heard *it*, he answered him, saying, Fear not: believe only, and she shall be made whole. 51 And when he came into the house, he suffered no man to go in, save Peter, and James, and John, and the father and the mother of the maiden. 52 And all wept, and bewailed her: but he said, Weep not; she is not dead, but sleepeth. 53 And they laughed him to scorn, knowing that she was dead. 54 And he put them all out, and took her by the hand, and called, saying, Maid, arise. 55 And her spirit came again, and she arose straightway: and he commanded to give her meat. 56 And her parents were astonished: but he charged them that they should tell no man what was done.

Note: Verse 55 says her spirit came again. She came from paradise and not hell.

Raising the Only Son of a Window

Luke 7:12 Now when he came nigh to the gate of the city, behold, there was a dead man carried out, the only son of his mother, and she was a widow: and much people of the city was with her. 13 And when the Lord saw her, he had compassion on her, and said unto her,

Weep not. 14 And he came and touched the bier: and they that bare *him* stood still. And he said, <u>Young man, I say unto thee, Arise</u>. 15 And <u>he that was dead sat up, and began to speak. And he delivered him to his mother.</u>

Note: So was the young man lost when he died? If he was he was in Hell. If he was in Hell, he was given a second chance out of Hell. No doubt he was saved and went to paradise. So if he was saved before he died and went to paradise and could lose his salvation, then when Jesus raised him from the dead He actually gave him another chance to be lost. This is a terrible thing to do to someone who was once in paradise.

Raising Lazarus

John 11:11 These things said he: and after that he saith unto them, Our friend Lazarus sleepeth; but I go, that I may awake him out of sleep. 12 Then said his disciples, Lord, if he sleep, he shall do well. 13 Howbeit <u>Jesus spake of his death</u>: but they thought that he had spoken of taking of rest in sleep. 14 Then said Jesus unto them plainly, <u>Lazarus is dead</u>. 15 And I am glad for your sakes that I was not there, to the intent ye may believe; nevertheless let us go unto him. 17 Then when Jesus came, he found that <u>he had *lain* in the grave four days already</u>. 23 Jesus saith unto her, Thy brother shall rise again. 24 Martha saith unto him, I know that he shall rise again in the resurrection at the last day. 25 Jesus said unto her, I am the resurrection, and the life: he that believeth in me, though he were dead, yet shall he live: 26 And whosoever liveth and believeth in me shall never die. Believest thou this? 27 She saith unto him, Yea, Lord: I believe that thou art the Christ, the Son of God, which should come into the world. 28 And when she had so said, she went her way, and called Mary her sister secretly, saying, The Master is come, and calleth for thee. 29 As soon as she heard *that*, she arose quickly, and came unto him. 30 Now Jesus was not yet come into the town, but was in that place where Martha met him. 32 Then when Mary was come where Jesus was, and saw him, she fell down at his feet, saying unto him, Lord, if thou hadst been here, my brother had not died. 33 When Jesus therefore saw her weeping, and the Jews also weeping which came with her, he groaned in the spirit, and was troubled, 34 And said, Where have ye laid him? They said unto him, Lord, come and see. 35 Jesus wept. 36 Then said the Jews, Behold how he loved him! 37 And some of them said, Could not this man, which opened the eyes of the blind, have caused that even this man should not have died? 38 Jesus therefore again groaning in himself cometh to the grave. It was a cave, and a stone lay upon it. 39 Jesus said, Take ye away the stone. Martha, the sister of him that was dead, saith unto him, Lord, by this time he stinketh: for he hath been *dead* four days. 40 Jesus saith unto her, Said I not unto thee, that, if thou wouldest believe, thou shouldest see the glory of God? 41 Then they took away the stone *from the place* where the dead was laid. And Jesus lifted up *his* eyes, and said, Father, I thank thee that thou hast heard me. 42 And I knew that thou hearest me always: but because of the people which stand by

I said *it*, that they may believe that thou hast sent me. 43 And when he thus had spoken, <u>he cried with a loud voice, Lazarus, come forth. 44 And he that was dead came forth,</u> bound hand and foot with graveclothes: and his face was bound about with a napkin. Jesus saith unto them, Loose him, and let him go.

Consider that these people that were raised from the dead were not lost people. If they were lost, Jesus brought them back from Hell, which would give them a second chance or a chance after death to be saved, which is contrary to the Bible teachings. So they were saved people that he raised from the dead. So they were brought back from paradise.

Now if you can lose your salvation, Jesus just gave them another opportunity to lose their salvation, which is a horrible thing to happen. The point again is that you cannot lose your salvation.

Chapter 6

The Matter of our Names
Written in Heaven

Luke 10:20 Notwithstanding in this rejoice not, that the spirits are subject unto you; but rather rejoice, because your names are written in heaven.

Note: If it is possible for your names to be removed or blotted out of the Lamb's Book of Life, why rejoice because it is there?

"The Book of the Living" and
"The Lamb's Book of Life"

Exodus 32:32 Yet now, if thou wilt forgive their sin--; and if not, blot me, I pray thee, out of thy book which thou hast written.

33 And the LORD said unto Moses, <u>Whosoever hath sinned against me, him will I blot out of my book.</u>

*Note: This verse is referring to "the book of the living" not the "Lamb's Book of Life". If it were referring to the "Lamb's Book of Life" no one would be saved because all have sinned. **Ecclesiastes 7:20** For <u>there is not a just man upon earth, that doeth good, and sinneth not</u>. Moses is offering for God to take his life, not his salvation. The particular ones that God is referring to are the men over 20 years old that will die* *in the wilderness. God is going to blot their names out of the "book of the living" because God is going to allow them to be killed.*

Psalm 69:28 Let them be blotted out of the book of the living, and not be written with the righteous.

Note: This verse proves that there are two different books. If it is an offer for the name to be blotted out this means that the name is already there. The name has to be there for it to be blotted out. This would be the book of the living. Then when there is the offer for the name not to be written, which means the name is not yet written there. It is referring to the second book, which is the Lamb's Book of Life.

    A.   *The book of the living*
    B.   *The Lamb's Book of Life*

The Lamb's Book of Life

Philippians 4:3 And I intreat thee also, true yokefellow, help those women which laboured with me in the gospel, with Clement also, and [with] other my fellowlabourers, whose names [are] in the book of life.

Written in the Lamb's Book of Life

Hebrews 12:23 To the general assembly and church of the firstborn, which are written in heaven, and to God the Judge of all, and to the spirits of just men made perfect,

Because of Trusting Christ as Savior We are Promised not to Have our Names Removed from the Lamb's Book of Life

Revelation 3:5 He that overcometh, the same shall be clothed in white raiment; <u>and I will not blot out his name out of the book of life</u>, but I will confess his name before my Father, and before his angels.

Note: We overcome by trusting Jesus as our Savior :

1 John 5:4-5 For whatsoever is born of God overcometh the world: and this is the victory that overcometh the world, *even* our faith. **5** Who is he that overcometh the world, but he that believeth that Jesus is the Son of God?

*Note: Here is God's promise that he will **not** blot our name out of the book of life.*

Revelation 13:8 And all that dwell upon the earth shall worship him, <u>whose names **are not** written in the book of life of the Lamb </u>slain from the foundation of the world.

Revelation 17:8 The beast that thou sawest was, and is not; and shall ascend out of the bottomless pit, and go into perdition: and they that dwell on the earth shall wonder, <u>whose names **were not** written in the book of life</u> from the foundation of the world, when they behold the beast that was, and is not, and yet is.

Revelation 20:12 And I saw the dead, small and great, stand before God; and the books were opened: and another book was opened, which is [the book] of life: and the dead were judged out of those things which were written in the books, according to their works.

15 <u>And whosoever was **not** found written in the book of life was cast into the lake of fire.</u>

Revelation 21:27 And there shall in no wise enter into it anything that defileth, neither [whatsoever] worketh abomination, or [maketh] a lie: but <u>they which are written in the Lamb's book of life</u>.

Revelation 22:19 And if any man shall take away from the words of the book of this prophecy, God shall take away his part out of the book of life, and out of the holy city, and [from] the things which are written in this book.

Note: This verse says "his part" not his name. God will remove his part or space where his name would have appeared out of the book of life. The warning applies to lost people. Saved people will not add to or take away from God's Word. The man that adds to or takes away from God's Word is sentenced to the Lake of Fire.

Sumary Facts:

1) There are two different books:

    *A. **The Book of the Living**: Every human being that has ever existed is written in this book, at the point of conception, with the promise of* being blotted out after they sin and die without being born again. (Ex. 32:33)

B. **The Lamb's Book of Life**: Every human being that is born again is written in this book, at the point of regeneration, with the promise never to be blotted out. (Rev. 3:5)

Chapter 7

<u>The Matter of Perfect Tense Verbs Used in the New Testament when Referring to Salvation</u>

Perfect tense in the Greek for verbs means "complete with results". It means an action that was completed in the past but has continuing results. It has no exact equivalent in English. It means once it is done it forever shall be done.

Notice the phrase "it is written" in the perfect tense means it was once written and will always be written.

Matthew 2:5 And they said unto him, In Bethlehem of Judaea: for thus ***it is written*** by the prophet,

Matthew 4:6 And saith unto him, If thou be the Son of God, cast thyself down: for ***it is written***, He shall give his angels charge concerning thee: and in *their* hands they shall bear thee up, lest at any time thou dash thy foot against a stone.

Matthew 4:4 But he answered and said, ***It is written***, Man shall not live by bread alone, but by every word that proceedeth out of the mouth of God.

Matthew 4:7 Jesus said unto him, ***It is written*** again, Thou shalt not tempt[a] the Lord thy God.

Matthew 4:10 Then saith Jesus unto him, Get thee hence, Satan: for *it is written*, Thou shalt worship the Lord thy God, and him only shalt thou serve.

Matthew 11:10 For this is *he*, of whom *it is written*, Behold, I send my messenger before thy face, which shall prepare thy way before thee.

Matthew 26:24 The Son of man goeth as *it is written* of him: but woe unto that man by whom the Son of man is betrayed! it had been good for that man if he had not been born.

Matthew 26:31 Then saith Jesus unto them, All ye shall be offended because of me this night: for *it is written*, I will smite the shepherd, and the sheep of the flock shall be scattered abroad.

Mark 1:2 As *it is written* in the prophets, Behold, I send my messenger before thy face, which shall prepare thy way before thee.

Matthew 21:13 And said unto them, *It is written*, My house shall be called the house of prayer; but ye have made it a den of thieves.

Mark 7:6 He answered and said unto them, Well hath Esaias prophesied of you hypocrites, as *it is written*, This people honoureth me with *their* lips, but their heart is far from me.

Mark 9:12 And he answered and told them, Elias verily cometh first, and restoreth all things; and how *it is* *written* of the Son of man, that he must suffer many things, and be set at nought.

Mark 9:13 But I say unto you, That Elias is indeed come, and they have done unto him whatsoever they listed, as *it is written* of him.

Mark 11:17 And he taught, saying unto them, Is it not *written*, My house shall be called of all nations the house of prayer? but ye have made it a den of thieves.

Mark 14:21 The Son of man indeed goeth, as *it is written* of him: but woe to that man by whom the Son of man is betrayed! good were it for that man if he had never been born.

Mark 14:27 And Jesus saith unto them, All ye shall be offended because of me this night: for *it is written*, I will smite the shepherd, and the sheep shall be scattered.

Luke 2:23 (As *it is written* in the law of the Lord, Every male that openeth the womb shall be called holy to the Lord;)

Luke 3:4 As *it is written* in the book of the words of Esaias the prophet, saying, The voice of one crying in the wilderness, Prepare ye the way of the Lord, make his paths straight.

Luke 4:4 And Jesus answered him, saying, *It is written*, That man shall not live by bread alone, but by every word of God.

Luke 4:8 And Jesus answered and said unto him, Get thee behind me, Satan: for *it is written*, Thou shalt worship the Lord thy God, and him only shalt thou serve.

Luke 4:10 For *it is written*, He shall give his angels charge over thee, to keep thee:

Luke 7:27 This is *he*, of whom *it is written*, Behold, I send my messenger before thy face, which shall prepare thy way before thee.

John 20:31 But these *are written*, that ye might believe that Jesus is the Christ, the Son of God; and that believing ye might have life through his name.

Acts 1:20 For it *is written* in the book of Psalms, Let his habitation be desolate, and let no man dwell therein: and his bishoprick[b] let another take.

Acts 7:42 Then God turned, and gave them up to worship the host of heaven; as *it is written* in the book of the prophets, O ye house of Israel, have ye offered to me slain beasts and sacrifices *by the space of* forty years in the wilderness?

Acts 13:33 God hath fulfilled the same unto us their children, in that he hath raised up Jesus again; as it is also *written* in the second psalm, Thou art my Son, this day have I begotten thee.

Acts 15:15 And to this agree the words of the prophets; as *it is written*,

Acts 23:5 Then said Paul, I wist not, brethren, that he was the high priest: for *it is written*, Thou shalt not speak evil of the ruler of thy people.

Luke 10:26 He said unto him, What *is written* in the law? how readest thou?

Luke 19:46 Saying unto them, *It is written*, My house is the house of prayer: but ye have made it a den of thieves.

Luke 24:46 And said unto them, Thus *it is written*, and thus it behoved Christ to suffer, and to rise from the dead the third day:

John 8:17 It is also *written* in your law, that the testimony of two men is true.

Romans 1:17 For therein is the righteousness of God revealed from faith to faith: as *it is written*, The just shall live by faith.

Romans 2:24 For the name of God is blasphemed among the Gentiles through you, as *it is written*.

Romans 3:4 God forbid: yea, let God be true, but every man a liar; as *it is written*, That thou mightest be justified in thy sayings, and mightest overcome when thou art judged.

Romans 3:10 As *it is written*, There is none righteous, no, not one:

Romans 8:36 As *it is written*, For thy sake we are killed all the day long; we are accounted as sheep for the slaughter.

Romans 9:13 As *it is written*, Jacob have I loved, but Esau have I hated.

Romans 9:33 As *it is written*, Behold, I lay in Sion a stumblingstone and rock of offence: and whosoever believeth on him shall not be ashamed[f].

Romans 10:15 And how shall they preach, except they be sent? as *it is written*, How beautiful are the feet of them that preach the gospel of peace, and bring glad tidings of good things!

Romans 11:8 (According as *it is written*, God hath given them the spirit of slumber[c], eyes that they should not see, and ears that they should not hear;) unto this day.

Romans 11:26 And so all Israel shall be saved: as *it is written*, There shall come out of Sion the Deliverer, and shall turn away ungodliness from Jacob:

Romans 12:19 Dearly beloved, avenge not yourselves, but *rather* give place unto wrath: for *it is written*, Vengeance *is* mine; I will repay, saith the Lord.

Romans 14:11 For *it is written*, *As* I live, saith the Lord, every knee shall bow to me, and every tongue shall confess to God.

Romans 15:3 For even Christ pleased not himself; but, as *it is written*, The reproaches of them that reproached thee fell on me.

Romans 15:9 And that the Gentiles might glorify God for *his* mercy; as *it is written*, For this cause I will confess to thee among the Gentiles, and sing unto thy name.

Romans 15:21 But as *it is written*, To whom he was not spoken of, they shall see: and they that have not heard shall understand.

1 Corinthians 1:19 For *it is written*, I will destroy the wisdom of the wise, and will bring to nothing the understanding of the prudent.

1 Corinthians 1:31 That, according as *it is written*, He that glorieth, let him glory in the Lord.

1 Corinthians 2:9 But as *it is written*, Eye hath not seen, nor ear heard, neither have entered into the heart of man, the things which God hath prepared for them that love him.

1 Corinthians 3:19 For the wisdom of this world is foolishness with God. For *it is written*, He taketh the wise in their own craftiness.

1 Corinthians 4:6 And these things, brethren, I have in a figure transferred to myself and *to* Apollos for your sakes; that ye might learn in us not to think *of men* above that which *is written*, that no one of you be puffed up for one against another.

1 Corinthians 9:9 For *it is written* in the law of Moses, Thou shalt not muzzle the mouth of the ox that treadeth out the corn. Doth God take care for oxen?

1 Corinthians 10:7 Neither be ye idolaters, as *were* some of them; as *__it is written__*, The people sat down to eat and drink, and rose up to play.

1 Corinthians 14:21 In the law *__it is written__*, With *men of* other tongues and other lips will I speak unto this people; and yet for all that will they not hear me, saith the Lord.

1 Corinthians 15:45 And so *__it is written__*, The first man Adam was made a living soul; the last Adam *was made*⁷ a quickening spirit.

2 Corinthians 8:15 As *__it is written__*, He that *had gathered* much had nothing over; and he that *had gathered* little had no lack.

2 Corinthians 9:9 (As *__it is written__*, He hath dispersed abroad; he hath given to the poor: his righteousness remaineth for ever.

Galatians 3:10 For as many as are of the works of the law are under the curse: for *__it is written__*, Cursed *is* every one that continueth not in all things which are written in the book of the law to do them.

Galatians 3:13 Christ hath redeemed us from the curse of the law, being made a curse for us: for *__it is written__*, Cursed *is* every one that hangeth on a tree:

Galatians 4:22 For *__it is written__*, that Abraham had two sons, the one by a bondmaid, the other by a freewoman.

Galatians 4:27 For *it is written*, Rejoice, *thou* barren that bearest not; break forth and cry, thou that travailest not: for the desolate hath many more children than she which hath an husband.

Hebrews 10:7 Then said I, Lo, I come (in the volume of the book *it is written* of me,) to do thy will, O God.

1 Peter 1:16 Because *it is written*, Be ye holy; for I am holy.

Notice the phrase "be forgiven" in the perfect tense means it was once forgiven and will always be forgiven.

Matthew 9:2 And, behold, they brought to him a man sick of the palsy, lying on a bed: and Jesus seeing their faith said unto the sick of the palsy; Son, be of good cheer; thy sins *be forgiven* thee.

Matthew 9:5 For whether is easier, to say, *Thy* sins *be forgiven* thee; or to say, Arise, and walk?

Mark 2:5 When Jesus saw their faith, he said unto the sick of the palsy, Son, thy sins *be forgiven* thee.

Mark 2:9 Whether is it easier to say to the sick of the palsy, *Thy* sins *be forgiven* thee; or to say, Arise, and take up thy bed, and walk?

Luke 5:20 And when he saw their faith, he said unto him, Man, thy sins *are forgiven* thee.

Luke 5:23 Whether is easier, to say, Thy sins *be forgiven* thee; or to say, Rise up and walk?

Luke 7:47 Wherefore I say unto thee, Her sins, which are many, ***are forgiven***; for she loved much: but to whom little is forgiven, *the same* loveth little.

Luke 7:48 And he said unto her, Thy sins ***are forgiven***.

1 John 2:12 I write unto you, little children, because your sins ***are forgiven*** you for his name's sake.

Notice the phrase "it is finished" in the perfect tense means it was once finished and will always be finished.

John 19:30 When Jesus therefore had received the vinegar, he said, ***It is finished***: and he bowed his head, and gave up the ghost.

Notice the phrase "he arose" or "risen" in the perfect tense means it was once risen and He will always be risen.

1 Corinthians 15:4 And that he was buried, and that ***he rose again*** the third day according to the scriptures:

1 Corinthians 15:12 Now if Christ be preached that ***he rose*** from the dead, how say some among you that there is no resurrection of the dead?

1 Corinthians 15:20 But now is Christ ***risen*** from the dead, *and* become the firstfruits of them that slept.

Notice the phrase "is born" in the perfect tense means he was once born again and will always be born again. So once a person is born again they will always and forever be born again.

1 John 2:29 If ye know that he is righteous, ye know that every one that doeth righteousness *is born* of him.

1 John 3:9 Whosoever is born of God doth not commit sin; for his seed remaineth in him: and he cannot sin, because *he is born* of God.

1 John 4:7 Beloved, let us love one another: for love is of God; and every one that loveth *is born* of God, and knoweth God.

1 John 5:1 Whosoever believeth that Jesus is the Christ *is born* of God: and every one that loveth him that begat loveth him also that is begotten of him.

Chapter 8

The Facts about Judas Iscariot in the Following Verses will Prove that Judas was Never Saved and Died and Went to Hell

Matthew 26:24 The Son of man goeth as it is written of him: but woe unto that man by whom the Son of man is betrayed! it had been good for that man if he had not been born.

Note: Because Judas was never saved Jesus said it had been good for him if he had not been born. Jesus would not be able to say that about Judas if he were ever saved.

Luke 22:3 Then entered Satan into Judas surnamed Iscariot, being of the number of the twelve.

John 13:27 And after the sop Satan entered into him. Then said Jesus unto him, That thou doest, do quickly.

*Note: If Judas was a saved man, it would be impossible for Satan to enter into him. Christians cannot be demon possessed. Notice **I John 4:4**. "Ye are of God, little children, and have overcome them: because greater is he that is in you, than he that is in the world." Notice **Matt. 12:29**. "Or else how can one enter into a strong man's house, and spoil his goods, except he first bind the strong man? And then he will spoil his house." Satan would first have to bind the Holy*

Spirit that dwells in the believer before he can possess the believer, but this is impossible.

Joh 6:64 But there are some of you that believe not. For <u>Jesus knew from the beginning who they were that believed not</u>, and who should betray him.

Note: Jesus knew Judas was an unbeliever.

John 6:70 Jesus answered them, Have not I chosen you twelve, and <u>one of you is a devil</u>?
<u>He spake of Judas Iscariot</u> *the son* of Simon: for he it was that should betray him, being one of the twelve.

Note: Jesus says Judas is a devil.

John 17:12 While I was with them in the world, I kept them in thy name: those that thou gavest me I have kept, and <u>none of them is lost, but the son of perdition; that the scripture might be fulfilled.</u>

Note: Jesus chose Judas knowing he was lost to fulfill scripture. Jesus said Judas is lost.

Chapter 9

What about People that Commit Suicide?

It is important to note that there are a number of believers in the Bible that wished for death at a very sad and low point in their lives. Example: **Jeremiah** in Jeremiah chapter 20; **Elijah** in I Kings 19; **Jonah** in Jonah 4; **Job** in Job chapter 3. Each wished and even tried to get God to kill them. They were in a very low and depressed point in their lives. None of these mentioned actually committing suicide even though the desire might have been there.

Now let us look in the Bible at the example of King Saul.

A. Saul's proof of being a genuine believer:

1 Samuel 10:9-10 And it was *so*, that when he had turned his back to go from Samuel, God gave him another heart: and all those signs came to pass that day. 10 And when they came thither to the hill, behold, a company of prophets met him; and the Spirit of God came upon him, and he prophesied among them.

B. Saul's death: 1 Samuel 31:1-6

1 Now the Philistines fought against Israel: and the men of Israel fled from before the Philistines, and fell down slain in mount Gilboa. 2 And the Philistines followed hard upon Saul and upon his sons; and the Philistines

slew Jonathan, and Abinadab, and Malchishua, Saul's sons. 3 And the battle went sore against Saul, and the archers hit him; and he was sore wounded of the archers. 4 Then said Saul unto his armourbearer, Draw thy sword, and thrust me through therewith; lest these uncircumcised come and thrust me through, and abuse me. But his armourbearer would not; for he was sore afraid. Therefore **Saul took a sword, and fell upon it**. 5 And when his armourbearer saw that Saul was dead, he fell likewise upon his sword, and died with him. 6 So **Saul died**, and his three sons, and his armourbearer, and all his men, that same day together.

C. Where did Saul go when he died? 1 Samuel 28:19

19 Moreover the LORD will also deliver Israel with thee into the hand of the Philistines: and <u>tomorrow *shalt* thou and thy sons *be* with me</u>: the LORD also shall deliver the host of Israel into the hand of the Philistines.

Note: The "thou" in this passage is referring to Saul. Samuel who is already in paradise is telling Saul that the next day Saul and his sons would be with him in paradise. The next day was the battle in which Saul was badly wounded and finally committed suicide. So from this example we see that suicide does not affect the destiny of your soul. However it will surely have an effect on your rewards or lack of rewards when you get to heaven.

Note: To suggest that Saul went to Hell here is ridiculous. To say that Samuel who was allowed to return from the dead and talk to Saul and tell him on the *next day your sons are going to be with me in Paradise but you will be in Hell is madness. Notice the warning again, "tomorrow shalt thou and thy sons be <u>with me</u>."*

A special note needs to be said about suicide. Sometimes we overlook the fact that many believers today are committing suicide slowly instead of instantly. We shutter at the thought of instant suicide but do not realize many of us are committing suicide slowly by sinful habits like using tobacco products or alcohol or drugs or attempting to live with unconfessed sin in our lives. Committing suicide is a terrible thing for anyone to do and is very wrong. Whether slowly or instantly it has no effect on their soul going to heaven but it has a huge effect on your rewards or reigning position in heaven. Even disobedience to our parents is a slow suicide. Note the following verses:

Ephesians 6:1-3 Children, obey your parents in the Lord: for this is right. 2 Honour thy father and mother; (which is the first commandment with promise;) 3 That it may be well with thee, and <u>thou mayest live long on the earth</u>.

Chapter 10

No Old Testament Saint was Saved by Works

Remember Satan's strategy. If Satan can get people to depend on something else besides Jesus and what He did for their salvation, Satan succeeds. ***Remember, Satan does not care what you depend on to get you to Heaven as long as it is not Jesus and what He did on the cross for us.***

Some people think that works and deeds such as animal sacrificing saved people in Old Testament times. With a close look at these verses, you can see that these individuals got saved the same as people in the New Testament times. They looked forward to the cross and Jesus dying for them and we look back to the cross and Jesus dying for us.

Act 10:43 To him give all the prophets witness, that through his name whosoever believeth in him shall receive remission of sins.

Acts 15:10 Now therefore why tempt ye God, to put a yoke upon the neck of the disciples, which neither our fathers nor we were able to bear?

11 But we believe that through the grace of the Lord Jesus Christ we shall be saved, even as they.

Acts 13:39 *And by him <u>all that believe are justified from all things, from which ye could not be justified by the law of Moses</u>.*

Hebrews 4:2 <u>*For unto us was the gospel preached, as well as unto them*</u>*: but the word preached did not profit them, not being mixed with faith in them that heard it.*

Hebrews 7:19 *For <u>the law made nothing perfect</u>, but the bringing in of a better hope did; by the which we draw nigh unto God.*

Hebrews 9:9 *Which was a figure for the time then present, in which were offered both <u>gifts and sacrifices, that could not make him that did the service perfect</u>, as pertaining to the conscience;*

Hebrews 10:1 *For the law having a shadow of good things to come, and not the very image of the things, <u>can never with those sacrifices which they offered year by year continually make the comers thereunto perfect.</u>*

Hebrews 10:4 <u>*For it is not possible that the blood of bulls and of goats should take away sins.*</u>

Hebrews 10:11 *And every priest standeth daily ministering and offering oftentimes the same sacrifices, <u>which can never take away sins:</u>*

Galatians 4:4 *But when the fulness of the time was come, God sent forth his Son, made of a woman, made under the law, **5**. <u>To redeem them that were under the law</u>, that we might receive the adoption of sons.*

Note: Do you get verse five: Jesus died to redeem them that were under the law.

Note: There was no law given that can bring salvation.

Galatians 2:21 *I do not frustrate the grace of God: for if righteousness come by the law, then Christ is dead in vain.*

Galatians 3:21 *Is the law then against the promises of God? God forbid: for if there had been a law given which could have given life, verily righteousness should have been by the law.*

a) Abraham

John 8:56 Your father Abraham rejoiced to see my (Jesus') day: and he saw *it*, and was glad.

Romans 4:1 What shall we say then that Abraham our father, as pertaining to the flesh, hath found? **2** For if Abraham were justified by works, he hath *whereof* to glory; but not before God. **3** For what saith the scripture? Abraham believed God, and it was counted unto him for righteousness.

Romans 4:9 *Cometh* this blessedness then upon the circumcision *only*, or upon the uncircumcision also? for we say that faith was reckoned to Abraham for righteousness.

James 2:23 And the scripture was fulfilled which saith, Abraham believed God, and it was imputed unto him for righteousness: and he was called the Friend of God.

Galatians 3:6 Even as Abraham believed God, and it was accounted to him for righteousness.

Galatians 3:8 And the scripture, foreseeing that God would justify the heathen through faith, <u>preached before the gospel unto Abraham</u>, *saying*, In thee shall all nations be blessed.

Genesis 15:6 And he believed in the LORD; and he counted it to him for righteousness.

Genesis 22:8 And Abraham said, My son, God will provide himself a lamb for a burnt offering: so they went both of them together.

b) David

Romans 4:6 Even as David also describeth the blessedness of the man, unto whom God imputeth righteousness without works, **7** *Saying*, Blessed *are* they whose iniquities are forgiven, and whose sins are covered. **8** Blessed *is* the man to whom the Lord will not impute sin.

Psalm 32:1 Blessed *is he whose* transgression *is* forgiven, *whose* sin *is* covered. **2** Blessed *is* the man unto whom the LORD imputeth not iniquity, and in whose spirit *there is* no guile.

c. Noah

Genesis 6:8 But Noah found grace in the eyes of the LORD.

Genesis 7:1 And the LORD said unto Noah, Come thou and all thy house into the ark; for thee have I seen righteous before me in this generation.

Hebrews 11:7 By faith Noah, being warned of God of things not seen as yet, moved with fear, prepared an ark to the saving of his house; by the which he condemned the world, and became heir of the righteousness which is by faith.

There are some people who are so convinced they can be saved by works that they will actually argue with God on Judgment Day at the White Throne Judgment using their works as an attempted defense thinking it will free them from Hell.

Matthew 7:22 Many will say to me in that day, Lord, Lord, have we not prophesied in thy name? and in thy name have cast out devils? and in thy name done many wonderful works? **23** And then will I profess unto them, I never knew you: depart from me, ye that work iniquity.

Chapter 11

What the Bible says about Chastisement

There are many who mock and joke about the doctrine of eternal security and produce statements such as these. If I believed in once saved always saved, I would go out and do anything wrong I wanted to do. Or once saved always saved gives a person a free ticket to sin. These people who say such things know nothing of God's chastening hand. Those who have honestly trusted Jesus Christ as their Savior are promised to receive chastisement from God for their own good if they sin against Him and do not apologize. Note the following verses.

Deu 8:5) Thou shalt also consider in thine heart, that, as a man **chasteneth** his son, *so* the LORD thy God **chasteneth** thee.

Note: See the following for the definition of chasteneth. "chasteneth" #3256 (43x)(chastise 21 instruct 8; correct 7; taught 2; bound; punish; reformed; reproveth; sore)
Note: As a father chastises his son, God chastises us.

2Sa 7:14-15) I will be his father, and he shall be my son. If he commit iniquity, I will **chasten** him with the rod of men, and with the stripes of the children of men:

15 But my mercy shall not depart away from him, as I took *it* from Saul, whom I put away before thee.

Note: "chasten" #3198 (59x)(reprove 23; rebuke 12; correct 3; plead 3; reason 2; chasten 2; reprover + <H376> 2; appointed; arguing; misc 9)

Job 5:17) Behold, happy *is* the man whom God correcteth: therefore despise not thou the chastening of the Almighty:

Note: "chastening" #4148 (50x)(instruction 30; correction 8; chasten 4; chastisement 3; check; bond; discipline; doctrine; rebuker)
Note: It is God who will correct us and chastise us when we do wrong.

Psalm 89:31 If they break my statutes, and keep not my commandments;

Psalm 89:32 Then will I visit their transgression with the rod, and their iniquity with stripes.

Psalm 89:33 Nevertheless my loving kindness will I not utterly take from him, nor suffer my faithfulness to fail.

Psalm 89:34 My covenant will I not break, nor alter the thing that is gone out of my lips.

Psa 94:12) Blessed *is* the man whom thou chastenest, O LORD, and teachest him out of thy law;

Note: "chastiseth" #3256 (43x)(chastise-21; instruct-8; correct-7; taught-2; bound; punish; reformed; reproveth; sore)

Pro 3:11) My son, despise not the chastening of the LORD; neither be weary of his correction:

1Co 11:32) But <u>when we are judged, we are chastened of the Lord, that we should not be condemned with the world.</u>

Note: "chastened" #3811 (13x)(chasten 6; chastise 2; learn 2; teach 2; instruct)

Note: When a person gets saved, their punishment for their sin changes from condemnation with the world which is Hell to the judgment of God which is chastisement in this life.

Heb 12:5) And ye have forgotten the exhortation which speaketh unto you as unto children, My son, despise not thou <u>the chastening of the Lord</u>, nor faint when thou art rebuked of him:

Heb 12:6) For <u>whom the Lord loveth he chasteneth, and scourgeth every son whom he receiveth.</u>

Heb 12:7) If ye endure chastening, God dealeth with you as with sons; for what son is he whom the father chasteneth not?

Heb 12:8) But if ye be without chastisement, whereof all are partakers, then are ye bastards, and not sons.

Note: If you get what is being said here, if a person has no chastisement for sin from God then God is not his Father. That person is lost. The person that claims that they are saved and can go out and do anything

wrong they want to do and nothing happens is a fake and still lost.

Hebrews 12:9 Furthermore we have had fathers of our flesh which <u>corrected *us*,</u> and we gave *them* reverence: shall we not much rather be in subjection unto the Father of spirits, and live?

Heb 12:10 For they verily for a few days chastened *us* after their own pleasure; but he for *our* profit, that *we* might be partakers of his holiness.

Heb 12:11 Now no chastening for the present seemeth to be joyous, but grievous: nevertheless afterward it yieldeth the peaceable fruit of righteousness unto them which are exercised thereby.

Rev 3:19) As many as I love, I rebuke and chasten: be zealous therefore, and repent.

Chapter 12

<u>What About Enduring to the End</u>

Matthew 10:22 And ye shall be hated of all *men* for my name's sake: but he that endureth to the end shall be saved.

Matthew 24:13 But he that shall endure unto the end, the same shall be saved.

Mark 13:13 And ye shall be hated of all *men* for my name's sake: but he that shall endure unto the end, the same shall be saved.

First we must realize that just because the word "saved" is used, it does not necessarily refer to salvation of the soul. For example:

Acts 27:20 And when neither sun nor stars in many days appeared, and no small tempest lay on *us*, all hope that we <u>should be saved</u> was then taken away.

Acts 27:31 Paul said to the centurion and to the soldiers, Except these abide in the ship, ye cannot <u>be saved</u>.

The above verses refer to being saved from a bad storm and referring to their natural lives not their souls.

1 Timothy 2:15 Notwithstanding she <u>shall be saved</u> in childbearing, if they continue in faith and charity and holiness with sobriety.

The above verse refers to being saved in child bearing or having a safe child bearing time. This is still a reference to the natural life and not the soul.

Jude 5 I will therefore put you in remembrance, though ye once knew this, how that the Lord, having <u>saved the people out of the land of Egypt</u>, afterward destroyed them that believed not.

The above verse refers to people being saved out of the land of Egypt and referring to the natural life and is not referring to the salvation of the soul.

Now back to the verses: **Mat.10:22; Mat. 24:13; and Mark 13:13**

Notice the verse following Mat. 24:13. Matthew 24:22 And except those days should be shortened, <u>there should no flesh be saved</u>: but for the elect's sake those days shall be shortened.

Notice it says in verse 22. "no flesh be saved". The term "saved" in Mat. 24:13 is a reference to the natural life not the soul.

Notice the verse following Mark 13:13. Mark 13:20 And except that the Lord had shortened those days, <u>no flesh should be saved</u>: but for the elect's sake, whom he hath chosen, he hath shortened the days.

Notice again it says in verse 20. "no flesh should be saved". The term "saved" in Mark13:13 is a reference to the natural life not the soul.

To suggest that the salvation of the soul requires us to endure to the end implies that salvation of the soul is not instant. From the previous verses and chapters in this book, we have seen many verses from the Bible that teach that salvation of the soul is instant. We receive eternal life immediately upon trusting Christ as our Savior. See again John 3:15; 16; 36; 5:24; 6:40; 6:47; I John 2:25; I John 5:13 and others.

Chapter 13

Requirements for Salvation versus Results of Salvation

Note: There are many who cannot see the difference between the requirements for salvation versus the results of salvation. If a person does not have the results of salvation, he must do the requirements for salvation. If he tries to do the results of salvation thinking this will save him, he is in for a frustrating and dangerous time in his life. The book of **I John** deals with many results of salvation issues which we will deal with in depth. First lets look at a few other passages of scripture that give examples of results versus requirements for salvation.

Requirements

Eph. 2:8 For by grace are ye saved through faith; and that not of yourselves: *it is* the gift of God:

Eph. 2:9 Not of works, lest any man should boast.

Results

Eph. 2:10 For we are his workmanship, created in Christ Jesus unto good works, which God hath before ordained that we should walk in them.

The above verses clearly tell us that works are not required for salvation in verses 8 and 9 but verse 10 tells us they are a result of salvation. Otherwise it will appear that verse 8-9 contradict verse 10. Remember if you do not have the results, do not go after the results. Go after the requirements and you will get the results.

Results

II Cor. 5:17 Therefore if any man *be* in Christ, *he is* a new creature: old things are passed away; behold, all things are become new.

Again the above verse is dealing with the results of salvation not the requirements of it. You do not make yourself a new creature to obtain salvation. Many are trying to make themselves a new creation to be saved or are trying to reform to be saved. God makes you a new creature when you trust Christ as your personal Savior and when He does all things will become new.

Now note the passages in I John:

Notice the passages on requirements for salvation.

1 John 2:22-23 Who is a liar but he that denieth that Jesus is the Christ? He is antichrist, that denieth the Father and the Son. *23* Whosoever denieth the Son, the same hath not the Father: *(but) he that acknowledgeth the Son hath the Father also.*

Note: Believing that Jesus is the Christ and believing in the Father and Son is one of the requirements for salvation.

1 John 4:2-3 Hereby know ye the Spirit of God: Every spirit that confesseth that Jesus Christ is come in the flesh is of God: *3* And every spirit that confesseth not that Jesus Christ is come in the flesh is not of God: and this is that *spirit* of antichrist, whereof ye have heard that it should come; and even now already is it in the world.

Note: Believing that Jesus came in human flesh is one of the requirements for salvation.

1 John 4:15 Whosoever shall confess that Jesus is the Son of God, God dwelleth in him, and he in God.

Note: Believing that Jesus is the Son of God is a requirement for salvation.

1 John 5:1 Whosoever believeth that Jesus is the Christ is born of God: and every one that loveth him that begat loveth him also that is begotten of him.

Note: Believing that Jesus is the Christ is a requirement for salvation.

1 John 5:10 He that believeth on the Son of God hath the witness in himself: he that believeth not God hath made him a liar; because he believeth not the record that God gave of his Son.

Note: Believing God and His Word is one of the requirements for salvation.

1 John 5:11-13 And this is the record, that God hath given to us eternal life, and this life is in his Son. **12** He that hath the Son hath life; *and* he that hath not the Son of God hath not life. **13** These things have I written unto you that believe on the name of the Son of God; that ye may know that ye have eternal life, and that ye may believe on the name of the Son of God.

Note: Having the Son as your Savior and believing on the name of Son of God is a requirement for salvation.

Notice the passages on the results of salvation.

1 John 2:3-5 And hereby we do know that we know him, if we <u>keep</u> his commandments. **4** He that saith, I know him, and <u>keepeth</u> not his commandments, is a liar, and the truth is not in him. **5** But whoso <u>keepeth</u> his word, in him verily is the love of God perfected: hereby know we that we are in him.

Note: The verbs (keep; keepeth; keepeth) are in the present tense which refer to continuous action. The person that freely disobeys God's commands without God's chastisement is not saved. Keeping the commands of God does not bring salvation. They are a result of salvation. You do not keep God's commands to get saved. You keep God's commands because you are saved. Because you have life from God you will keep God's commands. God's commands do not give life.

1 John 2:9-11 He that saith he is in the light, and <u>hateth</u> his brother, is in darkness even until now. *10* He that

<u>loveth</u> his brother abideth in the light, and there is none occasion of stumbling in him. *11* But he that <u>hateth</u> his brother is in darkness, and walketh in darkness, and knoweth not whither he goeth, because that darkness hath blinded his eyes.

Note: You do not love your brother to get saved. You love your brother because you are saved. The verbs (hateth; loveth; hateth) are in the present tense or continuous action. The person that can continually hate his brother without the chastening hand of God to correct him is lost.

1 John 3:6-8 Whosoever <u>abideth</u> in him <u>sinneth</u> not: whosoever <u>sinneth</u> hath not seen him, neither known him. *7* Little children, let no man deceive you: he that <u>doeth</u> righteousness is righteous, even as he is righteous. *8* He that <u>committeth</u> sin is of the devil; for the devil sinneth from the beginning. For this purpose the Son of God was manifested, that he might destroy the works of the devil.

Note: The verbs (abideth; sinneth; sinneth; committeth) are in the present tense or continuous action. Anyone who can continually sin against God without God's chastening hand to correct and stop him is lost.

1 John 3:9-10 Whosoever is born of God <u>doth</u> not <u>commit</u> sin; for <u>his seed remaineth in him: and he cannot sin</u>, because he is born of God. *10* In this the children of God are manifest, and the children of the devil: whosoever <u>doeth</u> not righteousness is not of God, neither he that <u>loveth</u> not his brother.

Note: The verbs (doeth commit; sin; doeth; loveth) are in the present tense or continuous action. Anyone who can continually sin against God without God's chastening hand to stop him is lost. This passage gives one of several reasons why a saved person cannot freely practice sin. Upon conversion he is given divine seed from God and cannot freely practice sin.

1 John 3:14-15 We know that we have passed from death unto life, because we <u>love</u> the brethren. He that <u>loveth</u> not *his* brother abideth in death. **15** Whosoever <u>hateth</u> his brother is a murderer: and ye know that no murderer hath eternal life abiding in him.

Note: You do not love your brother to get saved. You love your brother because you are saved. The verbs (love; loveth; hateth) are in the present tense or continuous action. The person that can continually hate his brother without the chastening hand of God to correct him is lost.

1 John 4:7-8 Beloved, let us love one another: for love is of God; and every one that <u>loveth</u> is born of God, and knoweth God. **8** He that <u>loveth</u> not knoweth not God; for God is love.

Note: You do not love in order to get saved. You love because you are saved. The verbs (loveth and loveth) are in the present tense or continuous action. The person that can continually hate without the chastening hand of God to correct him is lost.

1 John 4:20 If a man say, I <u>love</u> God, and <u>hateth</u> his brother, he is a liar: for he that <u>loveth</u> not his brother whom he hath seen, how can he <u>love</u> God whom he hath not seen?

Note: You do not love in order to get saved. You love because you are saved. The verbs (love; hateth; loveth and love) are in the present tense or continuous action. The person that can continually hate without the chastening hand of God to correct him is lost. The same heart that loves God will also love his or her brother. Verse 20 makes it clear that you cannot love God and hate your brother.

1 John 5:18 We know that whosoever is born of God <u>sinneth</u> not; but he that is begotten of God keepeth himself, and that wicked one toucheth him not.

Note: The verb (sinneth) is in the present tense or continuous action. Anyone who can continually sin against God without God's chastening hand to correct and stop him is lost.

3 John 1:11 Beloved, <u>follow</u> not that which is evil, but that which is good. He that <u>doeth</u> good is of God: but he that <u>doeth</u> evil hath not seen God.

Note: The verbs (follow; doeth; and doeth) are in the present tense or continuous action. Anyone who can continually sin against God without God's chastening hand to stop him is lost.

Note: With all the verses above in mind, now notice this verse. *1 John 1:10*

If we say that we <u>have</u> not <u>sinned</u>, we make him a liar, and his word is not in us.

Note: This verse makes it clear that we have all sinned but this verb phrase (have sinned) is not in the present tense or in continuous action. It is in the perfect tense which is completed action. The other passages we have dealt with are not saying that we cannot sin at all. If that were true no one could be saved. The other verses teach that as a result of salvation, God will not allow a believer to continually practice sin.

Chapter 14

<u>What about Blasphemy of the Holy Spirit</u>

Mark 3:28
Verily I say unto you, All sins shall be forgiven unto the sons of men, and blasphemies wherewith soever they shall blaspheme:

Mark 3:29
But he that shall blaspheme against the Holy Ghost hath never forgiveness, but is in danger of eternal damnation:

Matthew 12:31
Wherefore I say unto you, All manner of sin and blasphemy shall be forgiven unto men: but the blasphemy *against* the *Holy* Ghost shall not be forgiven unto men.

Note: The obvious question would be, what exactly is the "blasphemy of the Holy Spirit"? Consider the following:

Matthew 12:24-28
24 But when the Pharisees heard it, they said, <u>This fellow doth not cast out devils, but by Beelzebub the prince of the devils.</u>

25 And Jesus knew their thoughts, and said unto them, Every kingdom divided against itself is brought to desolation; and every city or house divided against itself shall not stand:

26 And if Satan cast out Satan, he is divided against himself; how shall then his kingdom stand?

27 <u>And if I by Beelzebub cast out devils</u>, by whom do your children cast them out? therefore they shall be your judges.

28 <u>But if I cast out devils by the Spirit of God</u>, then the kingdom of God is come unto you.

The Pharisees gave out the accusation that Jesus cast out devils by Beelzebub or Satan himself. Jesus made it clear that he cast out devils by the Spirit of God. Jesus then brought up the warning in Matt. 12:31 about "blasphemy of the Holy Spirit".

Note also the verse following Mark 3:28-29.

Mark 3:30 Because they said, He hath an unclean spirit. The scribes said that Jesus had an unclean spirit.

John 3:34 For he whom God hath sent speaketh the words of God: for God giveth not the Spirit by measure *unto him.*

Note: Jesus was not demon possessed, He was full of the Holy Spirit. With these passages we see the same accusation given this time from the scribes. **Mark 3:22** And the scribes which came down from Jerusalem said, <u>He hath Beelzebub, and by the prince of the devils casteth he out devils.</u>

Putting these together makes it is clear that the blasphemy of the Holy Spirit is accusing the work of the Holy Spirit to be of the devil. Example: The Bible was written by the Holy Spirit. (II Tim. 3:16) So, for someone to believe and say the Bible was written by the devil is an example of blasphemy of the Holy Spirit. Jesus cast out devils by the Holy Spirit but the scribes and Pharisees said Jesus cast out devils by Satan. This is another example of blasphemy of the Holy Spirit.

Now the next thing to consider is that whoever does this sin can never be forgiven and is hell bound. *Mark 3:29* But he that shall blaspheme against the Holy Ghost <u>hath never forgiveness, but is in danger of eternal damnation</u>: *Matthew 12:31* Wherefore I say unto you, All manner of sin and blasphemy shall be forgiven unto men: but <u>the blasphemy *against* the *Holy* Ghost shall not be forgiven unto men.</u>

Some have said that the blasphemy of the Holy Spirit is rejecting Christ as Savior. This cannot be true because many people rarely receive Christ as Savior the first time they hear the gospel. The blasphemy of the Holy Spirit has never forgiveness.

The next item to deal with is who can blaspheme the Holy Spirit. In the Bible the scribes and Pharisees were the ones who were blaspheming the Holy Spirit. The scribes and Pharisees were Christ rejecting lost sinners. They were religious but lost. Upon blaspheming the Holy Spirit they sentenced themselves to Hell.

Note: The following items are things that God will not allow a Christian to do.

1) The blasphemy of the Holy Spirit
2) Freely practicing sin without the chastening hand of God
3) Adding to or taking away from God's Word (Rev. 22:18-19)
4) Perverting the gospel of Christ itself. (Gal. 1:7-9)

Note: You have to ask yourself as a father, are there certain things that you would not allow your children to do? Of course there are many things we would stop our children from doing. God, who is the perfect Father, will not allow His children to do certain things either and is a far better father than us all. We might wonder about the freewill of the Christian. Consider the following passage.

1 Corinthians 6:19-20

19 What? know ye not that your body is the temple of the Holy Ghost *which is* in you, which ye have of God, and **ye are not your own**?

20 **For ye are bought with a price**: therefore glorify God in your body, and in your spirit, which are God's.

When you trust Christ as your Savior, you no longer belong to you. You belong to God. God becomes your Father and you are His child. There are certain things God will not allow you to do. There are also certain other things if attempted to continue to do will bring the chastening hand of God.

Chapter 15

Man's Righteousness versus God's Righteousness

Note: Every religion in the world can be put in to one of these two categories. The true religion is the one depending on God's righteousness and trusting Christ and what He did on the cross to save them. The other is the countless false religions that are depending on their own righteousness for their salvation and will be going to Hell.

First the verses on man's own righteousness:

Matthew 5:20 For I say unto you, That except your righteousness shall exceed *the righteousness* of the scribes and Pharisees, ye shall in no case enter into the kingdom of heaven.

Isaiah 64:6
But we are all as an unclean *thing*, and all our righteousnesses *are* as filthy rags; and we all do fade as a leaf; and our iniquities, like the wind, have taken us away.

Note: If our righteousness is as filthy rags, how much worse is our sin in God's eyes. Some are depending on the filthy rags of their own righteousness thinking this will get them to heaven.

Romans 10:5
For Moses describeth the righteousness which is of the law, That the man which doeth those things shall live by them.

Philippians 3:9
And be found in him, not having mine own righteousness, which is of the law, but that which is through the faith of Christ, the righteousness which is of God by faith:

Second the verses on God's righteousness imputed to man.

Romans 3:21
But now the righteousness of God without the law is manifested, being witnessed by the law and the prophets;

Romans 3:22
Even the righteousness of God *which is* by faith of Jesus Christ unto all and upon all them that believe: for there is no difference:

Romans 4:13
For the promise, that he should be the heir of the world, was not to Abraham, or to his seed, through the law, but through the righteousness of faith.

Romans 10:3-4
3 For they being ignorant of God's righteousness, and going about to establish their own righteousness, have not submitted themselves unto the righteousness of God.

4 For Christ *is* the end of the law for <u>righteousness to everyone that believeth.</u>

Romans 10:10
For with the heart man believeth unto righteousness; and with the mouth confession is made unto salvation.

Galatians 2:21
I do not frustrate the grace of God: for if righteousness *come* by the law, then Christ is dead in vain.

Galatians 3:21
Is the law then against the promises of God? God forbid: for if there had been a law given which could have given life, verily righteousness should have been by the law.

Chapter 16

What the Bible says about "carnal Christians"

Note: The term "carnal" used for the Christian is used very rarely in the Bible. As you will be able to see in the following verses, there are only five verses used for the term "carnal" when applied to the believer. **Let me make a statement up front that the true believer who gets carnal will not be able to stay carnal.** *It is true at the time when the believer is carnal, it is virtually impossible to tell them apart from a lost person. As has been stated elsewhere in this book, a true believer is going to have a hard time trying to stay carnal because God will chasten them or even take them home early by them dying a premature death. Lot would be a good example of a believer who lost everything he had because of his carnal ways. He tried his best to fit in with the wicked people of Sodom and could not. Notice the following passages:*

2 Peter 2:6-9

6 And turning the cities of Sodom and Gomorrha into ashes condemned them with an overthrow, making them an ensample unto those that after should live ungodly;

*7 And **delivered just Lot**, <u>vexed with the filthy conversation of the wicked</u>:*

*8 (For **that righteous man** dwelling among them, in seeing and hearing, <u>vexed his **righteous soul** from day to day with their unlawful deeds;</u>)*

9 The Lord knoweth how to deliver the godly out of temptations, and to reserve the unjust unto the day of judgment to be punished:

Let us examine the word "carnal".
"carnal" #4559 (11x)(carnal-9; fleshly-2)
"carnal" #4561 (151x)(flesh-147; carnal-2; carnally minded= <G5427>; fleshly)

There are other uses of the term "carnal" that are not attached to the believer himself. Romans 15:27 and I Corinthians 9:11 refer to carnal things as in material physical needs of the believers. II Corinthians 10:4 refers to the type of weapons a Christian can have, not physical or of this world but spiritual. Another application is in Hebrews 7:16 referring to a carnal commandment and Hebrews 9:10 referring to a carnal ordinance.

The passages we will deal with are in the verses below.

Romans 7:14
For we know that the law is spiritual: but <u>I am carnal, sold under sin</u>.

Note: Here Paul is giving a testimony to his own spiritual battle he has within of his sinful nature versus his divine nature. Note the following verse and testimony: **Romans 7:18** *For I know that in me (that is, in my flesh,) dwelleth no good thing: for to will is present with me; but how to perform that which is good I find not. Paul devotes almost the total of two chapters (6 & 7) of Romans to the battle he and every Christian has within themselves.*

Romans 8:7
Because the carnal mind *is* enmity against God: for it is not subject to the law of God, neither indeed can be.

Note: Here Paul makes a reference to the carnal mind of the believer that is enmity against God. It is a reference to the sinful nature in the believer that they have from birth with the divine nature given them upon trusting Christ as Savior. (II Pet. 1:4)

In I Corinthians another application to the term "carnal" is used to actually describe the believer's spiritual condition.

1 Corinthians 3:1
And I, brethren, could not speak unto you as unto spiritual, but as unto carnal, *even* as unto babes in Christ.

Note: Here Paul actually renames their spiritual condition. It is not only carnal but even "babes in Christ". There is an application to them being either *new converts and not yet growing and making progress or an application that they are believers who resist the normal process of growing as they should and are attempting to stay babies instead of growing up.*

1 Corinthians 3:3
For ye are yet carnal: for whereas *there is* among you envying, and strife, and divisions, are ye not carnal, and walk as men?

Note: The carnal condition puts forth the unholy fruit of envy and strife and brings divisions among other believers.

1 Corinthians 3:4 For while one saith, I am of Paul; and another, I *am* of Apollos; are ye not carnal?

Note: The carnal condition draws believers to follow men instead of Christ and this allows clicks to form in the assembly.
Note: Another reference to the believer's abnormal growth is in the following:

Hebrews 5:11-14 Of whom we have many things to say, and hard to be uttered, seeing ye are dull of hearing.

12 For when for the time ye ought to be teachers, ye have need that one teach you again which be the first principles of the oracles of God; and are become such as have need of milk, and not of strong meat.

13 For every one that useth milk is unskilful in the word of righteousness: for <u>*he is a babe*</u>.

14 But strong meat belongeth to them that are of full age, even those who by reason of use have their senses exercised to discern both good and evil.

Chapter 17

Access to God's Grace

Be aware that there are three access doors to God's grace and all three must be used at the same time to gain access to God's amazing grace.

1) Prayer or Asking

Hebrews 4:16
Let us therefore come boldly unto the throne of grace, that we may obtain mercy, and find grace to help in time of need.

2) Humility

James 4:6
But he giveth more grace. Wherefore he saith, God resisteth the proud, but giveth grace unto the humble.

1 Peter 5:5
Likewise, ye younger, submit yourselves unto the elder. Yea, all *of you* be subject one to another, and be clothed with humility: for God resisteth the proud, and giveth grace to the humble.

3) Faith

Romans 4:16
Therefore *it is* of faith, that *it might be* by grace; to the end the promise might be sure to all the seed; not to that

only which is of the law, but to that also which is of the faith of Abraham; who is the father of us all,

Romans 5:1-2
1 Therefore being justified by faith, we have peace with God through our Lord Jesus Christ:

2 By whom also <u>we have access by faith into this grace</u> wherein we stand, and rejoice in hope of the glory of God.

Now consider the following concerning Salvation.

Ephesians 2:8-9
8 For by grace are ye saved through faith; and that not of yourselves: *it is* the gift of God:

9 Not of works, lest any man should boast.

Acts 15:11
But we believe that through the grace of the Lord Jesus Christ we shall be saved, even as they.

About the three doorways: **Humility**: A person has to be humble enough to admit they are hell deserving sinners. A person has to be humble enough to admit they cannot save themselves. **Faith**: They must put their trust in Jesus and what He did for them on the cross to pay for their sins and depend on Jesus alone to save them. **Ask**: They must ask Jesus to be their personal Savior.

Romans 10:13 For whosoever shall call upon the name of the Lord shall be saved.

Now note the contrast: If a person attempts to put works into the plan of salvation, it totally does away with grace.

Romans 11:6 And if by grace, then *is it* no more of works: otherwise grace is no more grace. But if *it be* of works, then is it no more grace: otherwise work is no more work.

It would take a mighty proud person to think that there is anything they could do to help pay for their own sin. Knowing what the following passage says.

Isaiah 64:6 But we are all as an unclean *thing*, and <u>all our righteousnesses *are* as filthy rags</u>; and we all do fade as a leaf; and our iniquities, like the wind, have taken us away.

That is like offering God filthy rags to put with the blood of Christ to help pay for your sin. **<u>You can imagine how insulting that is to God.</u>**

Now consider the following warning in the passage of scripture:

Galatians 1:6-9

6 I marvel that ye are so soon removed from him that called you into the grace of Christ unto another gospel:

7 Which is not another; but there be some that trouble you, and would pervert the gospel of Christ.

8 <u>But though we, or an angel from heaven, preach any other gospel unto you than that which we have preached unto you, let him be accursed.</u>

9 As we said before, so say I now again, <u>If any *man* preach any other gospel unto you than that ye have received, let him be accursed.</u>

The danger of putting works into salvation is that instead of depending on Jesus and Him alone for your salvation, the individual is now depending on their own works to help save them or keep them saved. Remember Satan does not care what you are depending on to get you to heaven as long as it is not Jesus and what He did for us on the cross.

Chapter 18

What can a Christian Actually Lose?

A) One thing that a true believer can lose is his rewards.

Matthew 10:42 And whosoever shall give to drink unto one of these little ones a cup of cold *water* only in the name of a disciple, verily I say unto you, he shall in no wise lose his reward.

Mark 9:41 For whosoever shall give you a cup of water to drink in my name, because ye belong to Christ, verily I say unto you, he shall not lose his reward.

2 John 1:8 Look to yourselves, that we lose not those things which we have wrought, but that we receive a full reward.

First of all we need to examine what type of rewards God does give in heaven?

    a. **Crowns** (There are five crowns)

1 Corinthians 9:25 And every man that striveth for the mastery is temperate in all things. Now they [do it] to obtain a corruptible crown; but we an incorruptible.

1 Thessalonians 2:19 For what [is] our hope, or joy, or crown of rejoicing? [Are] not even ye in the presence of our Lord Jesus Christ at his coming?

2 Timothy 4:8 Henceforth there is laid up for me a crown of righteousness, which the Lord, the righteous judge, shall give me at that day: and not to me only, but unto all them also that love his appearing.

James 1:12 Blessed [is] the man that endureth temptation: for when he is tried, he shall receive the crown of life, which the Lord hath promised to them that love him.

1 Peter 5:4 And when the chief Shepherd shall appear, ye shall receive a crown of glory that fadeth not away.

Revelation 2:10 Fear none of those things which thou shalt suffer: behold, the devil shall cast [some] of you into prison, that ye may be tried; and ye shall have tribulation ten days: be thou faithful unto death, and I will give thee a crown of life.

Note: Notice the Bible here says a "crown of life" and not eternal life.

1) The Incorruptible Crown [I Cor. 9:25]
   A. Well disciplined

2) The Crown of Rejoicing [I Thess. 2:19]
   B. Soul winner's crown

3) The Crown of Righteousness [II Tim. 4:8]
   A. Love Christ's appearing

4) The Crown of Life [James 1:12; Rev. 2:10]
   A. Faithful unto death

    B. Endures temptation

    C. Loves God

5) The Crown of Glory [I Pet. 5:4]

    A. Pastors Crown

b. Reigning Positions

Matthew 25:21

His lord said unto him, Well done, *thou* good and faithful servant: thou hast been faithful over a few things, <u>I will make thee ruler over many things</u>: enter thou into the joy of thy lord.

Matthew 25:23

His lord said unto him, Well done, good and faithful servant; thou hast been faithful over a few things, <u>I will make thee ruler over many things</u>: enter thou into the joy of thy lord.

B) Another thing that can be lost by a true believer is the joy of their salvation.

Psalm 51:12 *Restore unto me the joy of thy salvation; and uphold me with thy free spirit.*

    King David got into sin and was chastised for it and in his confession in Psa. 51 he gave evidence that he had lost the joy of his salvation. Notice he did not say he lost his salvation but the joy of his salvation.

C) Another thing that can be lost by a true believer is their fellowship with God.

1 John 1:6 If we say that we have fellowship with him, and walk in darkness, we lie, and do not the truth:

1 John 1:7 But if we walk in the light, as he is in the light, we have fellowship one with another, and the blood of Jesus Christ his Son cleanseth us from all sin.

D) Another is there health.

1 Corinthians 11:28-33 But let a man examine himself, and so let him eat of that bread, and drink of that cup.

29 For he that eateth and drinketh unworthily, eateth and drinketh damnation to himself, not discerning the Lord's body.

> *Note: "damnation" #2917 (28x)(judgment 13; damnation 7; condemnation 5; be condemned; go to law + <u><G2192></u>; avenge + <u><G2919></u>)*
> *Note: The application of the word "damnation" here is explained in verse 32. The believer's judgment for sin is God's chastisement. It is not the condemnation with the world which is Hell.*

30 <u>For this cause many are weak and sickly among you,</u> and many sleep.

31 For if we would judge ourselves, we should not be judged.

32 But __when we are judged, we are chastened of the__
__Lord, that we should not be condemned with the world.__

33 Wherefore, my brethren, when ye come together to
eat, tarry one for another.

E. A believer can lose almost everything but he
cannot lose his salvation.

1 Corinthians 3:14-15

14 If any man's work abide which he hath built
thereupon, he shall receive a reward.

15 If any man's work shall be burned, he shall suffer
loss: but he himself shall be saved; yet so as by fire.

Chapter 19

Love versus Fear

1 John 4:18 There is no fear in love; but perfect love casteth out fear: because fear hath torment. He that feareth is not made perfect in love.

One of the problems with believing that there is a possibility of losing your salvation is the fear of just that, losing your salvation. The perspective that this forces people to live under is a great amount of fear and pressure. Every righteous deed that is done is done with the hope and fear that it is good enough to help save you or to help keep you saved. Consider the following and an entirely different and correct perspective of everything that you do provided you are depending on Jesus and what He did for you to pay for your sins on the cross to get you to heaven.

John 14:15 If ye love me, keep my commandments.

Jesus gives the ultimate motive for obedience. "LOVE" and not "FEAR".

1 John 5:3 For this is the love of God, that we keep his commandments: and his commandments are not grievous. (grievous meaning burdensome)

God even tells us why we love Him.

1 John 4:19 We love him, because he first loved us.

A person that has the assurance of their salvation and loves God will be the one that you cannot keep out of church. You will not be able to stop them from witnessing, giving, or reading their Bible, and praying. A study through time and history of every martyr for Christ had an amazing testimony by the persecutor when he voiced his thought at the moment of the murder of the saint. The one being martyred had an amazing love for God.

Even our children when they grow up enough to be obedient to their parents will enjoy their life more by being obedient to their parents because they love them and not because they fear a spanking for disobedience.

I have heard preachers who believe you can lose your salvation say they can cause their people to live holier and cleaner lives and get more service out of them because the preacher would tell them to beware lest they lose their salvation. My response is this. "Perfect love casteth out fear."

About the Author

Gerald McDaniel was born on June 26, 1954 in Pavo, Georgia. He was saved September 22, 1974. He answered the call to preach October 19, 1975. He was married in August of 1976 to Julie Kaye Ferguson of Covington, Indiana.

They have four children. Joanna, Josiah, Jonathan, and Joy. Joanna graduated from Pensacola Christian College in Florida. Josiah graduated from Georgia Southern University in Statesboro, Ga. Jonathan graduated from Darton College in Albany, Georgia and Valdosta State University in Valdosta. Joy graduated from Crown College in Powell, Tenn.

Gerald McDaniel has an Associate Degree in Engineering from Moultrie Technical College in Moultrie, Georgia. A Bachelor Degree from a combination of Hyles Anderson College of Indiana, Heritage Baptist College of Indiana and Andersonville Baptist Seminary and a Master's Degree at Andersonville Baptist Seminary in Georgia.

Gerald McDaniel has been a Pastor or Associate Pastor for over 35 years.